CAMBRIDGE LIBRARY COLLECTION

Books of enduring scholarly value

History

The books reissued in this series include accounts of historical events and movements by eye-witnesses and contemporaries, as well as landmark studies that assembled significant source materials or developed new historiographical methods. The series includes work in social, political and military history on a wide range of periods and regions, giving modern scholars ready access to influential publications of the past.

The Tea Industry in India

The origins of tea-brewing in India and China are still lost to history. In this 1882 guide to the Indian tea industry, Samuel Baildon (a tea-planter about whom little is known) describes some of the earliest theories and legends surrounding it, including both botanical speculations and the Chinese stories of Bodhidharma, the Indian monk said to have introduced tea to China and Japan. Well-versed in the investment opportunities of the Indian plantations, Baildon also provides a frank tour of the nineteenth-century industry. He includes advice for investors, who he insists must not try to assist the managers of their plantations, and for potential tea-planters, who he strongly discourages from the profession if they enjoy free time, reading, or friends. With specific and anecdotal accounts of the plantations written for newcomers to the trade, this candid guide now represents an invaluable resource for students of colonial history and agriculture.

T0300512

Cambridge University Press has long been a pioneer in the reissuing of out-of-print titles from its own backlist, producing digital reprints of books that are still sought after by scholars and students but could not be reprinted economically using traditional technology. The Cambridge Library Collection extends this activity to a wider range of books which are still of importance to researchers and professionals, either for the source material they contain, or as landmarks in the history of their academic discipline.

Drawing from the world-renowned collections in the Cambridge University Library and other partner libraries, and guided by the advice of experts in each subject area, Cambridge University Press is using state-of-the-art scanning machines in its own Printing House to capture the content of each book selected for inclusion. The files are processed to give a consistently clear, crisp image, and the books finished to the high quality standard for which the Press is recognised around the world. The latest print-on-demand technology ensures that the books will remain available indefinitely, and that orders for single or multiple copies can quickly be supplied.

The Cambridge Library Collection brings back to life books of enduring scholarly value (including out-of-copyright works originally issued by other publishers) across a wide range of disciplines in the humanities and social sciences and in science and technology.

The Tea Industry
in India

A Review of Finance and Labour,
and a Guide for Capitalists and Assistants

SAMUEL BAILDON

CAMBRIDGE
UNIVERSITY PRESS

CAMBRIDGE UNIVERSITY PRESS

Cambridge, New York, Melbourne, Madrid, Cape Town,
Singapore, São Paolo, Delhi, Mexico City

Published in the United States of America by Cambridge University Press, New York

www.cambridge.org
Information on this title: www.cambridge.org/9781108046244

© in this compilation Cambridge University Press 2012

This edition first published 1882
This digitally printed version 2012

ISBN 978-1-108-04624-4 Paperback

THE

TEA INDUSTRY IN INDIA.

A REVIEW OF FINANCE AND LABOUR,

AND A

GUIDE FOR CAPITALISTS AND ASSISTANTS.

BY

SAMUEL BAILDON,

AUTHOR OF " TEA IN ASSAM," ETC.

LONDON:

W. H. ALLEN & CO., 13 WATERLOO PLACE. S.W.

PUBLISHERS TO THE INDIA OFFICE.

1882.

LONDON
PRINTED BY W. H. ALLEN AND CO., 13, WATERLOO PLACE, S.W.

CONTENTS.

CHAPTER VII.

CHAPTER VIII.

THE

TEA INDUSTRY IN INDIA.

CHAPTER I.

INTRODUCTION.

THE *raison d'être* of any book ought to be that there is
room for it, and also that it is needed. It is in such a
belief that I have again ventured to seek the patronage
of those interested in the Indian tea industry; and I
may say that the belief rested, in the first place, on
the representation of a firm of London tea-brokers, that
such a book as I have now written would be of use at
the present time. Thinking over the remarks made in
this regard, I found that a wide field was open to me—
one that, so far as I was aware, had not been opened
up, and which, from the Indian side, it seemed to me,
could not very well be opened.

I thought, also, that if I could combine with (what I
hope is) an impartial view of the Indian tea industry,
information useful for the guidance of capitalists and
young men wishing to become tea-planters, I should be
supplying a want which I well knew existed. By the

1

kindness of Messrs. W. and R. Chambers, I am allowed to state, that various inquiries from different parts of the United Kingdom have been addressed to them on the subject of appointments, climate, openings for capital, &c., after the appearance in their *Journal* of short sketches of life in the Indian tea districts : which inquiries have been handed to me for reply. I have therefore striven to meet this want.

In reviewing my previous little work—*Tea in Assam*— the Editor of the Calcutta daily *Statesman* was kind enough to characterize it as "interesting." In my present endeavour I have remembered this, and have tried again to deserve such commendation. Class works are necessarily somewhat heavy in their reading : and knowing this, I have sought to make the subject as entertaining as was possible. This will explain the insertion of the chapters, "The Planter on Leave," and "The Social Phase of Tea-drinking." There is a great deal that is not cheerful in a tea-planter's life ; and I have consequently thought that a proven picture of the goal to which, I suppose, all men look—*i.e.* leave of absence— would perhaps act as a mental tonic to those that required one, and reconcile existing unpleasant-nesses by a cheerful hope for the future.

Since returning to England, some three years ago, I have continued my connexion with Indian tea. I think I may say, that in this time, and by the aid of know-ledge acquired in the Indian districts, I have been enabled to see some points, essential to the successful continuance of the industry, in a clearer light than could

be obtained by men wholly resident in India, either
through the medium of the press, or private correspondence. Planters naturally side with planters, agents
with agents, and owners with owners, when anything is
wrong ; each section believes in its own infallibility, and
in the error of the others ; and until they pass quite
out from either of the cliques mentioned, they must
continue to look upon most questions in a false light.
1 have found that many matters between the growers
of tea and its consignees here, need to be reconciled.
Also, that from want of a clearer knowledge of factory
management and agriculture, planters have been often
unjustly treated by Calcutta agents and London boards.
Equally, I have been compelled to believe, that for lack
of information, or consideration for the frequently
secondary position held by agents in India, planters did
not think quite as charitably as they might of their
employers, who were supposed sometimes to *dik* the lives
of managers, until existence—more particularly under
the well-known ethereal conditions of life in the Mo-
fussil—was not worth having. It is scarcely necessary
to say, that—especially in the present almost critical
state of the Indian tea industry—nothing could be more
detrimental to the common interest, than diverse, irre-
concilable opinions, which must inevitably result in
heartburnings, bickerings, and discord. It is surely a
need of the greatest magnitude, that there should be
perfect union and accord between the entire staff of each
interest ; because, if the owners and the agents, or the
agents and the planters, persist in pulling in different

1 *

directions, the interest must, as a natural sequence, suffer, or, more probably, fail altogether. I have endeavoured to show the individual interests at stake, and the expectations of each section of the management. In seeking to explain, and thereby remove, some of the obstacles to a more harmonious working, I have never lost sight of the fact that, however willing he might be, it was absolutely impossible for any one writer to make suggestions for the better management of an industry of the enormous extent of that of tea, and for him to be right upon every point. No one man could so thoroughly and completely grasp the situation; and I am far from wishing to set myself up as a re-organiser of what has been previously well organised by men far more capable than myself. Where a need of alteration has arisen, so far as I can see, it is through a change having occurred in the original order of things, when the organisation was equal to the occasion; but as in some cases, that need does not seem to have been altogether recognised, I have taken it upon myself, to the best of my ability, to point it out.

The labour question being one of, if not the most important considerations in some districts—and these the largest—I have tried to review the matter in its entirety, showing the errors which exist, and a means of remedying them. While I do not expect an unqualified acceptance of my suggestions, I certainly hope that some definite action may result from them.

In endeavouring to prove that in India, and not

China, the tea-plant has its home, I know I have written matter which, in itself, cannot result in any *tangible* good to the Indian tea industry. But the present age is essentially one of discovery in research ; and if India can be proved—as I hope I have proved it—to be the home of the tea-plant, Indian planters will have a strong base-point on which to reasonably establish their assertion as to the superiority of their produce. And I think I shall not be insinuating weakness, if I say that the industry on which I write needs all that can be said in its favour. It is as yet only a child, striving against the Chinese giant ; but, fortunately, the natural order of things is for the giants to die before the vigorous children.

There will be found in the following pages, I think I may say necessarily, a good deal of a personal pronoun of the first person singular. Its use has been avoided wherever possible, but there is plenty of it remaining, nevertheless. I mention this, lest any reader should think I am not aware of the fact.

In the course of my work I have felt that the extent of the subject written upon was considerable ; but no point has been advanced without careful consideration. I therefore hope that my work will result in the establishment of a better understanding between parties concerned in the tea industry, where it can be established, and that the suggestions made will, in some instances at all events, prove serviceable.

CHAPTER II.

INDIA THE HOME OF THE TEA-PLANT.

DOUBTS have been expressed in the last few years as to the accuracy of the general belief that the tea-plant had its home in China.

It must be admitted to be rather late in the day now to advance theories as to the nativity of a plant whose cultivation has been carried on for centuries; at the same time there will be nothing lost by looking into such records as exist, to see what information can be obtained on the subject.

Theorists are always eminently convincing to themselves; so in the present case, I know one individual who feels quite sure—no matter how general or ancient be the belief to the contrary—that India is the natural home of the tea-plant.

Ball, in his exhaustive and valuable work, *The Cultivation and Manufacture of Tea*, says (p. 15), "It may be here proper to remark that on the authorities of certain Japanese authors, a doubt has been raised by the Dr. Von Siebold, an intelligent botanist some years resident in Japan, as to the tea-plant being indigenous in China. All are agreed that it is of exotic growth in Japan, and was introduced into that country from China in the sixth century, agreeably to Kaempfer, or the ninth century (which seems more probable), according to Von Siebold."

The early history of the tea-plant is surrounded by the cloudy legends and mythological narratives of the imaginative Chinese. One writer says, " The origin of the use of tea, as collected from the works of the Chinese, is traced to the fabulous period of their history. . . . The earliest authentic account of tea, if anything so obscure and vague can be considered authentic, is contained in the *She King*, one of the classical works of high antiquity and veneration amongst the Chinese, and compiled by their renowned philosopher and moralist, Confucius. . . . In this treatise (*Kuen Fang Pu*), in the article " The Ancient History of Tea," an absurd story is related of the discovery of this tree in the Tsin dynasty. In the reign of Yuen Ty, in the dynasty of Tsin, an old woman was accustomed to proceed every morning at day-break to the market-place, carrying a small cup of tea in the palm of her hand. The people bought it eagerly ; and yet from the break of day to the close of evening, the cup was never exhausted. The money received, she distributed to the orphan and the needy beggar frequenting the highways. The people seized and confined her in prison. At night she flew through the prison window with her little vase in her hand."

Another (legendary) version of the origin of the tea-plant, is, that in or about the year of grace 510, an Indian prince and religious devotee named Dharma, third son of King Kosjusva, imposed upon himself, in his wanderings, the rather inconvenient penance of doing without sleep. The little Chinese narrative says that the Indian gentleman (who must have differed vastly from his countrymen of the present day), got on very comfortably for some years; until all at once he gave up, and had forty winks on a mountain-side. Upon awakening, Dharma was so grieved to find that he could not move about for years without going to sleep, that he pulled out his eye-lashes and flung them on the ground. Coming round that way later on, he found the offending lashes had grown into bushes, such as he had never before seen; and his long ignorance of sleep not having taken all the curiosity out of him, he nibbled the leaves, and found them possessed of an eye-opening tendency. He related the discovery to his friends and neighbours, and the tea-plant was forthwith taken in hand.

This, the most generally accepted indication of the first notice of tea in China—vague and legendary, I admit, but nothing more accurate is obtainable—uses the name of Dharma as the promoter or creator of the tea-plant. The actual records speak positively of such a man, saying he was a native of India, probably a Fakir, and that he crossed to Japan. Kaempfer states upon the authority of the Japanese chronicles, that tea was introduced into that country by a prince of the name of Dharma.

It will be advancing no theory to say that many mythological legends are based upon actual occurrences. In this year of enlightenment, 1881, we do not, of course, believe that a man named Dharma—especially an Indian—lived for years without sleeping, any more than we do that the tea-plant came out of his head; but it is possible, and even very probable, that the plant was brought to the notice of the Chinese by Dharma, just as it was to that of the Japanese by the same person. And when the ancient history of China is studied, one is quite prepared to find that a matter of past discovery or introduction has been enshrouded in a fanciful record verging upon, if not actually clothed in, the allegorical, while at the same time indicating the actual. Yet, do what we will, we are, of course, guided by conjecture; by reason of which, at this late date, it is difficult either to prove or deny the existence of the tea-plant in China anterior to, or through the agency of Dharma.

Briefly, the matter stands thus. The most feasible of the Chinese *legends* on the subject, makes the existence of the tea-plant in China to have originated with Dharma, who came from India in A.D. 510. The Chinese *chronicles* tell of such a visitor during the reign of Vû Ty, A.D. 543, stating that he came from India and crossed to Japan. The Japanese chronicles record the visit, and say Dharma introduced the tea-plant to that country. The Chinese and Japanese versions of the first phases of tea in their respective countries are thus attributed to a native of India. If we enter into the conjectural domain of " perhaps," there will scarcely be a limit to surpassing whatever we may advance. I will therefore venture only one " perhaps," and I feel quite sorry to do even that, having no doubt that Dharma was a very respectable individual, when doing the tea-plant business in China, at the time that England was divided into several kingdoms.

My one " perhaps " is this; and I think all who understand the Indian character at the present time will admit that it is not a far-fetched one. Perhaps Dharma, finding he was introducing to the Chinese an unknown plant, possessing peculiar properties, accounted for its existence in true Oriental fashion in a way not lowering to his own importance in the eyes of a superstitious people.

Mr. Ball says (p. 17), " Recent discoveries in Assam also seem to justify the assumption, if nothing to the contrary be known, that it (tea) has spontaneously extended its growth along a continuous and almost uninterrupted mountainous range, but of moderate altitude, nearly from the great river the Yang-ese-Kiang, to the countries flanking the south-western frontier of China, where this range falls in with, or, agreeably with the opinion of a well-informed and scientific author, Dr. Royle, forms a continuation of the Himalayan range. But in those countries, as in every part of China, if found in the plains or in the vicinity of habitations and cultivated grounds, it may be fairly assumed that it was brought and propagated there by the agency and industry of man."

There is neither a record, nor anything approaching a reasonable legend, to prove that tea was discovered in a wild state in China before Dharma brought it to notice. The earliest mention tells of people using it, and it may be inferred therefrom that they cultivated it. Precise and accurate information is obtainable as to the actual discovery of tea in Assam, *away* from habitations, and in dense jungles, far from " cultivated grounds." But similar information is not obtainable in connexion with the first days of tea amongst the Chinese. We may reasonably suppose that the place in which nature plants anything is better suited to its growth than a chance one of man's selection, and also that nature does not plant a shrub in a place of medium suitability, and leave it " spontaneously to extend its growth " into a more fitting spot many hundreds of miles distant. And as to the suitability of India for tea, there can be no question ; for even what is known as the Chinese plant gives a better return in India than in its reputed native land. We may either dispense with the agency of Dharma altogether, as having introduced the plant to China from India, or just reverse Mr. Ball's theory, and suppose that instead of the plant being indigenous to China and extending its growth along the countries mentioned into India, that it was indigenous to India, and extended its growth to China, *deteriorating as it did so.*

Taking India as the real home of tea, there was, of course, primarily, but one kind of plant. But I am reminded, in thus writing, of the botanical classification of the *Thea viridis,* and the *Thea bohea.* I was recently

informed by a well-known professional botanist, that it is
still almost an open question as to what is the difference
between the two plants ; and that there is no doubt as
to their having originally been one and the same. In
India, making either green or black tea depends upon
the will of the planter.

But all writers on Indian tea have been obliged to
give three classes of the plant—the indigenous, the China,
and the hybrid ; though according to the theory I have
mentioned, the China plant is but a deteriorated specimen
of the pure (Indian) plant.   But centuries of varied
cultivation in a climate not its own, and no small
amount of neglect, have made this wandering offshoot a
distinct variety, although ranking botanically partly
under the same name as its parent, *Thea bohea* ; so
distinct, indeed, as to have assisted in the production of
an entirely new plant—the Hybrid.

We will put this degenerated Indian tea-plant of
China, in its origin, in the position of a traveller ; and,
remembering that plant-life is more easily influenced by
climate than human life, suppose that an European was
cast upon the world, and travelling gradually farther and
farther from his native land, eventually settled down
in a climate altogether unsuitable for his successful
development. After the lapse of a great number of years,
he would nominally remain an European, but virtually
be an established member of another community, and
affected by habits of life, climatic influences, and intimate associations with things and people around him.
His nationality would have been abandoned for the

adoption of that of an inferior country, and have resulted in his decline. In the course of time we see him—or his progeny—stunted, changed, coarse, in every way degenerated ; in fact, changed physically from his original state.

So with China tea : originally part of the one Indian family, now a distinct and separate member.

In the early days of the tea enterprise in India, in-digenous plants were collected and formed into gardens, and China plants, propagated from seed, were planted in close proximity to the Indian species. The Chinese plants, having entirely changed from what they were in their origin, in the botanical course of nature imparted their altered condition, in some degree, to other plants around them ; and the very obvious result of planting two kinds of tea came about in the production of a third —the hybrid. From the small proportion of China plant originally placed in the experimental gardens, we see the wonderful blending of nature, in the fact that very little purely indigenous, or purely China, tea, remains—the various tea-producing districts in India almost all growing hybrid bushes. There are sections of a few — I was almost saying two or three—estates in Assam, where indigenous plant is cultivated exclusively ; and the greatest care is taken to keep all China and hybrid plants out of the way, so as to ensure the continued purity of species.

But Indian tea is now almost entirely of the hybrid class, of various degrees. What little remains of the originally propagated China tea, is a scrubby bush, with numerous small branches growing directly from the earth, and bearing hard, stunted leaves. Take this, as a wandering member of its family and the outcome of neglected cultivation in an inferior climate, and the imagination can easily picture what a specimen well-nourished in its natural soil is like. Tall, vigorous, of increased stature, with larger leaves, and full of sap ; giving a greater return, and of a richer kind.

The introduction of China tea (in seed) into India, has frequently been deplored, as the plant is not a particularly remunerative one to cultivate. But few evils are devoid of some indirect good ; and although the China specimen is a disagreeable thing to grow, and its out-turn more generally unsatisfactory than otherwise, the hardy nature it has blended with the pure Indian plant is a very wholesome addition.

China tea is a wandering member of a respectable family. It originally belonged to a delicately nurtured household, which received from nature all it needed, was looked after by the same generous parent, and consequently throve. But it went away from its native spot, and at last settled down in China Its new home was not so good ; and its requirements, not being so well supplied, had to be curtailed, to its own physical detriment. In short, China tea has " roughed it " ; and in returning to its native place—India—force of habit and years of privation have rendered the old needs necessaries no longer. It has become accustomed to a seemingly insufficient rainfall ; blight attacks but does not kill it ; coolies occasionally hack its laterals with the hoe, and women sometimes reduce its recently increased stature with no very gentle hand; novices also treat it unkindly with the pruning-knife, and the Borer gets at him. But he can bear all these things, after enduring what the pigtails in China called "tea cultivation." Having escaped, and returned to his native land, he imparts some of his hardened endurance to the family, puts a little of his sluggish blood and toughened body into theirs, and so renders them less finely strung, less delicate, and better able to bear the freaks of society without injury.

It is more satisfactory to cultivate good hybrid than either indigenous or China plants. The blended natures have resulted in a vigorous and hardy specimen, more suited to the climates in which it has been planted, than is the pure Indian variety, yet retaining a sufficiency of its original character to make its culture remunerative. A good tea climate must be humid. The atmosphere in the forest home of the Assam tea-plant is sometimes so moist as almost to give the idea of solidity. Hidden in the jungles where the rain fell in torrents, and where the dense undergrowth prevented the sun from drying up the ground, the tea-plant originally lived in an atmosphere which was always damp. But it was discovered in its wild luxuriance, protected by almost impenetrable jungle; and British energy and enterprise brought it out of seclusion. It was taken away and planted in open spaces, deprived of the shelter of its giant neighbours, and exposed to the direct action of the sun; and having a supply of moisture only when it rained, it forgot how to vegetate as it previously had. So it was found that what had been healthy and vigorous as jungle, was apt to be delicate and fragile as a cultivated plant. It is because of this, that the propagation of the alien (China) plant, has not been without its good. The sturdy, sluggish nature of the Indo-Celestial species, has blended harmoniously and advantageously with the pure Indian variety ; and what was absolutely necessary for the successful extension of the Indian tea industry— a plant more prolific than the China, yet less delicate than the indigenous—nature has bountifully given in the hybrid.

Confining, for the moment, my remarks to the province of Assam, the immense extent which the tea industry has assumed has changed, or, perhaps I should say, modified, the climate of the district. Not a great many years ago, there was a large tract of country several hundred miles in length, lying between two ranges of hills in the Bengal Presidency, through which a mighty river ran, which was supposed to have its source right away north of the Himalaya mountains ; but beyond this, very little was known. The place was Assam — governed by a Rajah and his ministers, and to which neither railway nor steamers went. It gradually came into notice after its annexation from the Burmese in 1826 ; but the era of its opening out and becoming generally known commenced in 1838 with the tea enterprise. It was the Inferno of Bengal ; a place to which but few people went, and from which even fewer returned ; humid and deadly, with jungle, fevers, ague, and tigers, holding supreme sway. What is Assam now ?

I might almost say a smiling province. The erstwhile unopened stretch of country between two ranges of hills and intersected by a river, is now a fairly cultivated district, sending its produce all over the world ; giving employment to hundreds of Europeans and thousands of natives ; communicated with (in part) by the railway of the Eastern Bengal Company, and the steamers of two companies ; boasting of its importance in the possession of a Chief Commissioner, and an Administration separate from that of the Bengal Presidency. Where once jungle and its deadly miasma concealed the riches and importance of the province, hundreds of thousands of acres of open land are now to be seen, planted with tea ! Compared with past times, Assam is no longer a howling wilderness ; and the change from hundreds of miles of waste into cultivated land has altered almost everything. Therefore, as I have said, the climate has become greatly modified. It needs no argument to support the fact that where you clear and cultivate land the rainfall is lessened ; and the atmospheric moisture is reduced when the sun gets to the earth, and the soil is sweetened by ventilation and good cultivation. To the tea-plant in its wild state, moisture was most essential ; but extended cultivation has reduced the humidity of Assam, and the indigenous plant is consequently not so well off when cultivated as when in its jungly seclusion.

Tea of the hybrid class is being cultivated remuneratively at the present time in places where, I am certain, the indigenous plant could not live. Tea of the same

2

order is also thriving and paying, after living through neglect and harsh treatment which would have killed indigenous tea in its infancy. Had the deteriorated (China) plant not been brought back to India, and allied itself with its old species, I am convinced that the enterprise of *Indian* tea cultivation would have been confined to a very considerably less extent than that at which it is now carried on. Assam is acknowledged to be the best tea climate in India ; yet even here, in many places, indigenous tea will not thrive. What, then, about other districts with climates less favourable than Assam ? Unless China tea had been introduced for exclusive growth in such localities, there would have been no plants suitable for them. It is hardly to be expected that results obtained from China gardens in Kangra and Kumáon would have been sufficient to increase the industry to its present dimensions. The indigenous Indian plant was found growing in rich soil, in valleys sheltered by dense jungles and with a very moist atmosphere ; and it would be unreasonable to expect it to thrive, if even to live, on exposed hilly elevations and in drier climates out of Assam. The natural inference, therefore, is, that districts now growing tea would not have been opened out as tea-producing districts, but for the happy provision of nature in supplying a suitable plant. Suffering indirectly from John Chinaman's ill-treatment, it was well off when fairly cultivated in moderately good soil, and receiving a medium rainfall. It did not languish or grow delicate when away from jungly seclusion and constant moisture ; so it was planted in many districts of India and in Ceylon, and is doing well every-where.

Thea Bohea Assamica went away from home, and allowed botanists (who had not found his parents), to give him the name of *Chinensis* ; but he has gone back now to the old country, and has agreed to remain, upon the acceptance of the equitable proposition (resulting from these radical times), that as he and his near relatives are getting old it is useless to quarrel about the family name ; so they have made a new one, of a modern cast, for their progeny, which writers on the subject designate in English instead of afflicting it with its doubtful Latin title, and call the hybrid. There is peace in the family at last, and the rising generation is looked upon hopefully.

2 *

CHAPTER III.

THE SUPERIORITY OF INDIAN OVER CHINA TEAS.

In Chapter II. " India the Home of the Tea-plant," I have endeavoured to show that as a growing plant Indian tea is superior to that of China. The most natural sequence would therefore be that the manufactured produce would be better—and so it is.

I have also elsewhere mentioned the purpose to which Indian tea is put by the retailing grocer; and I think the simple fact that it is systematically used to fortify tea from China, will decisively prove it to be generally superior for practical purposes. My wish, in this chapter, is to show by what causes, other than the fact of the tea-plant being in its natural home in India, this superiority is brought about and maintained.

The chemical constituents of good tea are the volatile oil, tannic acid, and theine, with other such elements as are commonly found in the leaves of vegetables. It

owes its smell, and part of its effects, to its volatile oil.
The tannic acid blackens the salts of iron, as does the
tannic acid of the oak. The theine is the most remarkable constituent. In using tea, those parts only are
used which are extracted by the water—the ethereal oil,
the tannate of theine, gum, and most of the soluble
salts. The theine is composed of eight atoms of
carbon, four atoms of nitrogen, ten atoms of hydro-
gen, and two atoms of oxygen ; and the nutritive power
is contained in the two azotised substances—theine and
caseine.

Such is good tea. In Chapter VIII. " The Social Phase
of Tea-drinking," will be found some of the beneficial
effects ; but to show its possible action upon the system,
I quote from the work of one of the most eminent
medical authorities, Dr. Thompson :—

" There is probably no substance, not strictly medicinal,
which exerts so powerful an influence upon the nervous
system as tea, especially the green variety, of which many
individuals cannot even take the smallest quantity without
experiencing the most disagreeable effects ; they become
faint, the action of the nervous system is disturbed,
the hand trembles, the heart palpitates, sometimes
gastric spasm is induced, but more generally a feeling of
raking the stomach, and of extreme hunger after a full
meal ; lastly, there is extreme wakefulness. There are
some persons upon whom green tea produces the same
effect as digitalis, and it has been medicinally employed
in the diseases for which that herb has so deservedly
obtained a high reputation. Desbois, of Rochefort, has,

by the use of it, cured many nervous diseases which have arisen from accelerated circulation. Dr. Percival had an idea that green tea possessed nearly the same power as digitalis of controlling and abating the action of the heart. It is upon the nervous system that the effects of tea are chiefly manifested ; green tea especially is distinguished by this property. It is said that a strong solution of it applied to the sciatic nerve for half an hour has caused death. Introduced in only a small quantity below the abdominal integuments of a frog, it produced complete paralysis of its hind legs, lasting for some hours. Administered as an injection to a dog, it caused a perfect paralysis of the bladder and intestinal sphincters, a partial loss of power in the hind legs, and a total loss in the tail. A poultice of green tea-leaves applied on the human stomach has caused sickness and vomiting ; over the abdomen, colicky pains and purgings; over the heart, faintness and irregularity of pulsation ; over the kidneys, diæresis. True, these are chiefly the results of green tea, but, on some, black tea will produce nearly the same symptoms. Where individuals have any tendency to dyspeptic affections, they are very apt to be aggravated by the use of tea, which occasions severe gastralgia.''

These are the occasional effects of presumably good tea. What need be said of the possible results of the adulterated kinds ?

I will now give an extract from a work on China tea by Mr. Samuel Ball.

'' There can be no doubt that the tea-shrub is very

extensively cultivated in China ; and the probability is, that every province, by means of its sheltered valleys, is enabled to contribute largely to its own domestic consumption. *Still, the ground allotted to the growth of this shrub being commonly only such as is unproductive, hilly, or otherwise unprofitable, as the banks of arable and cultivated grounds ;* and as every part of the empire is not equally favourable to its growth, it has often been questioned how far the use of this refreshing beverage is within the daily reach of the lowest order of the people. It is, without doubt, extensively used by all classes of the community, even the lowest, in some form or other, throughout this vast country ; *but it is equally certain that innumerable other leaves are employed as substitutes by many people among the poorer class, as frequent experience shows.* I examined many samples of such tea brought down to Canton by the gentlemen connected with Lord Amherst's embassy. Long lists of plants, moreover, are found in many of the Chinese herbals, to which the same term, ' tea,' is applied; though the Chinese very well distinguish the pure tea from its substitute, by observing that the plants so used, ' though they bear the name of tea, are not of the tea species.' *In fact, they use the term ' tea ' in a general sense, as we do, to signify any infusion of leaves."*

On the testimony of the House of Commons, " millions of pounds of sloe, liquorice, and ash leaves, are every year mixed with Chinese teas for England." It is well

* The italics are added.

known that the leaves of the Charrapal, a Californian bush, are largely exported to China, whence they return packed under the title of tea.*

So much for the spurious vegetable basis of adulteration. Mr. Fortune, in his interesting work, shows up the "facing" process, of making up once-used leaves with the aid of Prussian blue, silica, gypsum, plumbago, lamp-black, ferruginous earth, and other abominations. A Chinese journal says on the subject :

"The wonder is that such stuff should be suffered to be manufactured, much less to be shipped as a lawful export, for Chinese law expressly prohibits the re-manipulation of tea that has once been used, on the obvious and common-sense principles that such a trade is necessarily, in its very essence, fraudulent. Yet in the face of this well-known maxim, it is one of the thousand proofs which we have of the utter rottenness of the present administration, that all around the settlement, in every convenient open space, large quantities of what is termed, with ominous propriety, "the mixture," lie exposed to the sun at noon-day, in some cases within a hundred yards of the Mixed Court zamen. And not only so, but there are the establishments, well known to the police, where the mixture is fired, leaded, packed, sold, and despatched for shipment ; and experience has shown that it is useless to expect conviction, under Chinese law, from a Chinese magistrate."

The same journal, referring to a peculiar kind of

---

* *Food Papers*, by S. P. Day.

willow which grows abundantly in the country, the leaves of which are utilised by tea manufacturers, observes :

" One needs not the expensive craft of the cha-sze to know how neatly a little skilful manipulation, and a little heat applied *secundum artem*, can transform these willow leaves into genuine and delicate tea-leaves. Whether the mercantile result be intended to astonish the palates of old ladies in London or Glasgow, or to pass as genuine Souchong with skippers who have little knowledge of tea, we know not; but the fact remains, that the trade thrives well, and pays."*

A startling exposure was made a few years since, of the tea-rubbish styled " Finest New Season Kaisow " and " Fine Oanfa Congou," sold in bond at 1¼d. to 1¾d. per lb. Upon analysis, the former was found to contain an enormous amount of mineral matter, chiefly iron filings; while the latter proved a mixture of re-dried tea-leaves, straw, fragments of matting, rice-husks, willow leaves, and the excrement of silkworms. The " Maloo Mixture," likewise, once gained an unenviable notoriety, as did the " Extra Fine Moyune Gunpowder," put up for sale by auction in Mincing Lane, and in which Dr. Letheby discovered 40 per cent. of iron filings and 19 per cent. of silica. Some years since, the City Commissioners made a commendable but abortive effort to seize " Lie Tea," and teas artificially coloured and otherwise adulterated ; but inasmuch as duty had been

* *Food Papers.*

paid on the rubbish, it was found that nothing could be
done to arrest the distribution of such vile stuff.*

There will have been often noticed in China tea a
very strong aroma, which, although pleasant to the
smell, makes the infusion (especially when it has cooled)
of a rather sickly taste. Mr. Ball says on this subject:—

" The Chinese seem universally to agree, in ancient as
in modern times, that no factitious scent can be given to
tea which at all equals its natural fragrance; in short,
they say that ' only common tea requires scenting.'
Those persons who have had an opportunity of drinking
some of the finest kinds of Souchong tea will perhaps
agree with the Chinese in this opinion. There are,
however, many scented teas, which, so far from being
inferior, are even costly, and much esteemed both in
China and in Europe. Of these the Chu Lan, or
Cowslip Hyson, may be considered the best. I shall
therefore now explain the manner in which I have seen
this process performed; which, indeed, does not differ
greatly from that in practice 900 years ago, as described
in the *Keun-Fang-Pu*, a Chinese herbal. The flowers
may be gathered at any time of the day, but those
are considered the best and most fragrant which are
gathered while the dew is yet on the leaves.

" The tea about to be scented must be taken hot
from the last roasting, which immediately precedes the
packing, and poured into a Hyson chest so as to form a
layer of two inches in height from the bottom. A

* *Food Papers.*

handful or more of the fresh flowers, already separated from the stalks, is then strewed over the tea. In this manner the tea and flowers are placed in layers until the chest is quite full. The mouth of the canister is then closed, and the tea thus remains twenty-four hours. The proper proportion is three catties of flowers to 100 catties of tea. The next day the chest is emptied, when the tea and flowers are mixed together. They then undergo the process of Poey, about three catties being put in one sieve. The Poey Long is completely closed, and the tea and flowers are thus roasted from about one to two hours, or, rather, until the flowers become crisp. The flowers are then sifted out, and the tea packed. If the tea requires any further scenting, fresh flowers must be used, and the process repeated as before. The method of Poey is the same as that used for the black tea, only that the bottom of the sieve is covered with thin paper. The tea thus prepared is then mixed with other tea in the proportion of one part of scented tea to twenty of plain. The whole is then slightly heated in a Kuo (Chao), and when packed constitutes the description often denominated in England Cowslip Hyson.* Tea may be scented at any time with this kind of tea, but it must be previously heated or roasted about two hours.

" The mode of scenting black tea differs from that of green ; and, so far as I understand, there are two or three methods of performing this process. The Sonchy

---

* No wonder.

or Caper teas, the Tex Siong, and other teas of the
cowslip flavour, are also scented with the Chu Lan
flower (*Chloranthus inconspicuus*).

"After gathering, the flowers are separated from the
stalks as before, when some people dry them in the
sun ; but the best mode is to dry them in a Poey Long
over a slow fire, taking care not to change the yellow
colour of the petals.   When dried, they are put aside to
cool, and are afterwards reduced to a powder.   If this
powder, the scent of which is very powerful, be sprinkled
over the leaves previously to the last or two last
roastings and rollings in the process of Poey, the tea
will be highly scented ; but this is an expensive mode,
on account of the additional quantity of flowers required,
and therefore is seldom practised.   The usual mode is
by sprinkling a small quantity of this powder over the
tea during the last process of Poey, which takes place
previously to packing.   A small white powder, frequently
found in black teas of the caper flavour, cannot have
escaped the observation of the tea-dealers in England.
This powder is that of the Chu Lan flower, whose
colour has been changed to white in the process of
Poey.

"There is another scented tea of excellent flavour,
which is made in small quantities, and occasionally
sent to foreigners as presents.   This is a Souchong
tea, scented with the flower of the Pac Sheem (*Gardenia
florida*).

"There are two other scented teas, also of fine flavour,
both Souchong teas, the one scented with the Quy-fa

or Kuey-hoa (*Olea fragrans*), and the other with the Moo-Ly-Hoa (*Jasminum Sambac*).   Some people say that these three last teas are mixed with the flowers, as the Hyson tea is mixed with the Chu Lan, and are scented in the same manner.   But others say that two sieves are placed in the Poey Long, the lower one containing the flowers, and the upper one the tea.   The latter is the mode in which the Pac Sheem tea, to which I have previously alluded, is scented.   These are all the flowers with which I am acquainted, which are employed to scent tea ; but in the *Kuen-Fang-Pu* and *Quang-Tong-Chy* (or Canton Geographical History) many others are enumerated as eligible for that purpose."

Such is the decoction prepared at no little labour and expense by the " heathen Chinee."   Taking it as true that " good wine needs no bush," surely good tea that is not deficient in volatile oil does not need the perfume of other flowers.   It is impossible not to agree with the Chinese observation recorded by Mr. Ball, that " only common tea requires scenting."   An instance of the injurious effects of this foreign aroma was given me recently by a gentleman lately resident in Assam, in the Public Works Department.   When staying at the sea-side, it was his custom (Indian fashion) to let a cup of tea remain over from breakfast to be drank when reading the morning paper.   But regularly every morning, shortly after taking it, he experienced a feeling of the most nauseous sickness.   Not being particularly well at the time, he not unreasonably supposed that his liver was unpleasantly reminding him of India, and medicine was taken; but the feeling of sickness continued to occur every day, and on mentioning the circumstance to his family, he found they all suffered with the same complaint. Thereupon the tea-caddy was investigated, and its contents were found to be of a highly aromatic and very pleasant odour. Next morning no tea was used, and no sickness occurred; on the following one it was again tried, with the same unpleasant results as before. On the same day an order was sent to London for Indian tea.

At the recent exhibition in Sydney, the Chinese teas subjected to a Government analysis were pronounced, in many instances, to be adulterated with injurious, and in some cases even poisonous, matters, while in the Indian exhibits, placed under the same test, *not one case of adulteration was recorded.*

Against these many charges of the injurious adulteration of Chinese teas, as far as I can anywhere ascertain, I believe that there is, if any, only one case on record —and that of a long time ago—of anything approaching adulteration of Indian tea. Every pound that is offered for sale in England can be *guaranteed as absolutely pure.* This is its reputation with the trade; and in the course of a very large number of enquiries, the only deviation from this general belief in its purity, was an easily explained remark, that in some of the broken teas, occasionally small pieces of charcoal were found.

I happened recently to be speaking with the captain of a sailing vessel who had just reached home after a protracted voyage. In telling me how he had had to signal to a passing ship for provisions, he said that the tea given them " was strong Indian stuff that they couldn't drink, and when diluted sufficiently not to rasp their tongues (having no milk), it was unpleasantly insipid."

The very lowest price realised for Indian tea is considerably above the *minimum* obtained for that from China ; the former is therefore of a higher standard and of greater value than the latter.

Sir Walter Midhurst, the British Consul at Shanghai, not long ago stated in an official report :—

" We have to look to India for the perfection of tea-culture ; there planting, firing, and packing, are all in one hand, and the needful capital outlay to produce a good result is not spared. In China these desiderata are absent altogether, and the proceeds are in the primitive and unscientific style dear to the natives of this country. Nothing, it may be safely advanced, but the introduction of European capital and enterprise into the tea districts, will save the foreign tea trade of China from decay."

This local opinion of the Chinese tea industry is corroborated by some of the authorities in Mincing Lane, who, while not anticipating the collapse of the China tea trade, believe that India, possessing all essentials to success, will be able in the course of time to take the lead, provided always that those engaged in the industry work steadily and thoroughly, and upon sound principles of agriculture and finance.

The value of Indian tea, in addition to its known

purity, is also upheld by its great strength. Mr. Ball
says on this subject : " Strength and astringency are
more important qualities in tea than flavour ; and the
Assam tree seems to possess these in an eminent
degree."

Another cause of the superiority is seen in the different ways in which the whole enterprise is conducted in
the two countries. In China, as has been shown, people
are not particular as to the kind of land in which they
plant tea ; beside which, the cultivation is carried on
almost exclusively by natives. The tea-plant is farmed
by the Chinese. Families have little patches, and make
the most they can out of them. Some sell their green
leaf, others make the tea and sell that. When the leaf
is gathered and sold to a buyer, it is very probably sold
again to someone else ; but while it is passing from one
to the other in this way, it is deteriorating every hour.
Or when the grower of the tea manufactures it, he sells
it to a buyer of made tea, who passes it to another, and
so on ; and often tea passes in baskets through five or
six hands to the sea-port, and is then packed. Large
dealers buy up tea, and put it aside until they have a
sufficiency of the kind for final sale : and the time that
elapses between the plucking of the leaf and the
packing of the tea is most indefinite. When the
grower of the leaf has sold it, or the tea made from
it, he has quite done with it : and what afterwards
becomes of it concerns him not in the least. He probably has an idea that the man who bought it from him
will sell it to someone else; it possibly occurs to him as

he whiffs his evening pipe of opium, that what has been
grown in his garden will be put on a ship and go a long
distance : but whether it will turn out good or bad, or
show a loss or a profit, is nothing at all to him. All
he has to do is to grow more leaf. How differently
matters are conducted in India ! Instead of putting tea
into the ground, as a last resource to get something to
grow on it, Indian planters are anxious to obtain the best
possible soil for their seed. The entire enterprise in
India is under European supervision. In China, as a
rule, the shipper knows nothing of the spot on which his
merchandise was grown ; and provided he realises well,
it is no matter to him whether the grower cultivated his
plants properly or not. In India, from first to last,
producing the crop and hearing of its sale is the care
and anxiety of one man. He selects his land, clears
and plants it. He may be working for himself or for
others ; but he gives his entire care and attention to
everything connected with his crop—gathering, manufacture, packing, and despatch—and considers himself
responsible for it all. Even when the tea has left him
he has not done with it, and he waits anxiously for
particulars of its sale. If the tea be faulty, there is no
getting out of it ; as errors of manufacture never escape
the London brokers. The Indian planter cannot afford
to treat lightly anything in connexion with the tea from
his estate ; and I may safely say that he has no wish to
do so. The consequence is, that Indian tea is most carefully grown, manufactured, and despatched. Nothing
can be worse than to delay the manufacture of tea, or to

let it lie about, as is the case in China. An Indian planter's most earnest wish is to manufacture his crop as soon after plucking as can be done with safety, and to despatch it as soon after manufacture as possible.

Indian tea, therefore, is superior to Chinese tea as a growing plant; as a manufactured article, it suffers less deterioration, is infinitely purer, and needs, and has, no artificial doctoring to make it presentable; its intrinsic value is greater; without it a very large proportion of the present China imports would be unsaleable; when offered for sale side by side with China tea, it enjoys the confidence of the buyer in a far greater measure than the latter does, and   competed for as a pure, economical, and useful article   consumption.

CHAPTER IV.

INDIA AND TEA-PLANTERS.

DURING the last few years, the Indian tea districts have come to the notice of people in England, satisfactorily in a two-fold measure—as a field for capitalists, and as a working sphere for many young fellows who could not get into the right thing at home. In both respects, circumstances have shown up several things favourable to tea and India. Town residents in England who have looked to other countries for openings for capital, have been unable to see in Australia, New Zealand, or America a satisfactory field, because nearly all mediums of investment rendered some particular knowledge necessary to begin with, or else their capital was virtually placed under the control of other people. As one of the London journals recently said, it seems rather late in the day for a man of say 24 or 25, after being used to town life only, to go to America, or to the Colonies, to begin to learn the principles of farming or stock-raising. Most of the openings for capital in the Colonies are in

3 *

land ; and it is risky, or, at all events, unsatisfactory, to invest without at least a fair knowledge of the industry entered upon. Where a man has been a dweller in cities all his life, he is likely to obtain only a secondary knowledge of occupations so exacting as farming or stock-raising. Then, too, it is generally expected that anyone who goes in for agriculture in the Colonies will himself do the work of at least one man ; but willingness to do this will not produce the muscle and sinew necessary. Then, as to non-capitalists. There are many young fellows in England who are of such an active temperament as to rebel at the prospect of an indoor life, and who, from the same cause, have been unable to settle down to the study necessary to a profession. They have not felt good enough for the Church, not studious enough for the Bar, and although they might have managed to pull through the years necessary to the practice of medicine, and eventually pass, they would do so only to find themselves lacking the capital which is generally requisite for a fair professional beginning. Studying for the higher grades of Government service has been too severe for their fancy ; clerkships in Banks or Public Companies, obtainable through influence, have seemed the only openings available, and even those of but poor prospect as regarded the future.

For many such, the Indian tea districts have solved the problem of what to do. A tea-planter's life is very active, without giving any quantity of actually manual labour ; but some of the duties of the vocation are of a nature which renders it necessary that a man should be a good correspondent and book-keeper, and also have a clear, well-balanced head, to enable him to grasp the situation of factory administration in all its many bearings.

I have received from Messrs. W and R. Chambers, of Edinburgh, several requests for information as to the tea-planter's profession; and I now wish to set the whole matter plainly before the English reader, so that he may be able to decide whether he is a fit man to go to India, and also whether India is worth going to. I shall hope to put out the entire subject in a truthful, unbiassed light, from a strictly general point of view, and not merely from the way in which tea-planting agreed or disagreed with myself. I also hope to be able to represent matters fairly for capitalists and workers.

It will be a safe thing to begin by noticing the romance which, in the minds of people out of it, surrounds India even now. The results of the marvellous accounts brought home by the first representatives of John Company in India, and supported by the gorgeousness of the wealth of later arrivals, have seemingly been to fix on the minds of the British public the idea that, notwithstanding its heat and its fevers, India is still a grand country of vast and easily-obtainable wealth, of tigers, and shawls, and jewels, and elephants, and palaces, and bungalows, and missionaries, and funeral piles, and snakes, and heathens, and—well, ever so many other things, strange and peculiar. With the exception of the wealth and (perhaps) the funeral pile (*Suttee*), the other things are true; but to the Anglo-Indian mind they are not surrounded in any way by a halo of romance, such as conceals their unpleasantnesses from people at home.   As for the wealth, the time has passed for people to stand beneath the silver-tree in the moonlight and whistle for the rupees to come down.   The princely fortunes of a century ago have become very rare things indeed at the present time; and natives no longer pay their respects to various high officials with a *salaami* of a plateful of gold Mohurs.   (It is generally oranges or bilious sweetmeats in the tea districts.)   To people out of official service at home, India at this time stands—or ought to stand—in some respects, in the light of an undeveloped country in which money is to be made by steady work and a sufficiency of capital to start with. India, for Europeans, has changed altogether from the old-time order of things—even from that which ruled sixty years ago.   For then Europeans went to India with the intention of settling there; it was indeed a " farewell " they gave on leaving home; and they often remained away, without a visit, until they were able to return for good.   They consequently became far more Indian, and far less English, than do men at this time. There were fewer English people in India, and fewer English things; the *dâk gharry* served for the railway; there was no telegraph, nor ice-machines in the plains; Green's liners went and came round the Cape, and the mails could not then reach London from Calcutta in twenty-three days.   Western habits and Western social observances have become comparatively general in India, and the consequence is that English people remain essentially English, and feel that with the Suez Canal and the Mont Cenis Tunnel, home is close at hand. The splendour of the native princes has well-nigh died out of India, and the romance surrounding English life has also gone ; and there remains a country near to England, although differing in itself, where Englishmen manage pretty successfully to live in a way that (with the exception of the numerous servants) fairly well resembles life in their own land. I purposely review European life in India thus, in the hope of preventing young fellows going to the country only to have all the fallacious glory and romance suddenly knocked out of them, on commencing housekeeping in a tea-district bungalow.

Now, it is, of course, a very essential thing that only the right kind of men should become tea-planters, both for their own sakes, and also for that of the industry. Farther on I shall show what kind of life is led on tea-plantations, and the reader will be able to determine whether he is the right kind of man for such a life. I may safely say that people who are well fitted for indoor occupations, and dislike the idea of an outdoor one, should never seek positions on tea estates ; and that those who find themselves comfortable and happy in sedentary occupations should keep to them. It would be wrong to say that good mercantile men (or office men generally) cannot become good tea-planters ; but I would advise all men who feel themselves well fitted for office life to keep to it. While I know some who have become competent planters, I also know others who have made complete failures. Now there are periods in the life of almost every man, especially when he is young, in which circumstances make him think that some mode of life other than that in which he is engaged would be far more pleasant and satisfactory. Office men, as they sit in black coats over their desks in the summer, think of the free and easy life of men in America or the Colonies (or the Indian tea districts), where people "ride about all day long in their shirt-sleeves, and never wear a collar." They think this must be very jolly. Or, perhaps, as they travel homeward after the work of the day, in the face of a biting east wind, receive a small pellet of thawing snow down the back from the hand of a wicked boy who hides himself round the corner, they think how much jollier it would be if they lived in a warmer climate, where the east wind was not so keen, the boys not so wicked, and where it did not snow at all. And in the bright beauty of early spring, when Nature is brilliant after the dreariness of the winter, they think, as they bend over ledgers, how preferable would be a walk amongst the fresh-budding trees, and a ramble in the country; in fact, how much better altogether would an outdoor life be than an indoor one. Mercantile London is almost a nautical community during the summer holidays. The residents of towns often have as great a wish to live in the country as country people have to reside in towns—neither can see much beauty in their surroundings. But the book-keeper would probably fail, physically and mentally, in a farmer's work, and the farmer would want to return to his horses and turnips when put to book-keeping. Men who are well fitted for office life should keep to it, because that fitness generally carries with it a train of appreciation for other occupations which have no place—or scarcely any—in a tea-planter's life. "Let the cobbler stick to his last."

Shortly before I went to India I was fortunate in being advised on several points by a Doctor from the tea districts; and, amongst other things, he told me to take out all mediums of resource for occupying leisure that I might possess—musical instruments, paint-boxes, drawing materials, &c., as if I had leisure, and nothing to occupy it, I should be in a bad way. Accordingly I took flutes, a concertina, paint-boxes, as many books as I could get, and a multitude of odds and ends, together with an intention to be most industrious in utilising my leisure; but when I had settled down in my quarters, I found I had scarcely any opportunities for using the preventatives of idleness with which I had provided myself. It was possible to read just a little in bed at night, under a mosquito-curtain; and it was also possible to try to charm snakes and jackals in the vicinity with strains which I believed were musical. But playing "Home, Sweet Home" on a flute, as a mosquito begins a *piano* passage near your ear, with a *crescendo* movement as it approaches the nose, and a *forte finale* as it settles on the tip thereof, and in a bungalow that is solitary, save for the rats and bats, is not a cheerful occupation; and the strains of a concertina seem to be strangely

wanting in something, if you happen to look outside
into the night, and see the silent jungle all around
you.   It is in every way advisable to have some
resources for leisure, should the chance fall to your
lot ; but if a man has been in the habit of depending
upon settled methods of occupying his spare time, or
upon different social mediums for completing the
happiness of his life, he had better not go to the tea
districts ; for if he does, his existence is likely to seem
something very like a curse to him.   Men who are
socially active at home in literary, musical, debating, or
similar societies, or who are of a regularly studious turn,
who like to read and study in the winter evenings, and
take quiet strolls in search of botanical or geological
specimens, or perhaps to reason out more clearly some
theory that needs adjustment, during the summer, had
far better remain in England than go to the Indian tea-
plantations.   And others who love the Sabbath because
of its quiet peace, and rest, and spiritual exercises, or
are active members of choirs or Sunday Schools, had
also better remain in England ; or their life will be
one long regret and wish to return.   After the novelty
of being in a new country has passed away, they will
find themselves face to face with the hard fact that
everything that was most congenial to them has been
given up, and that they have reached a country
in which all the under-currents of pleasant, gentle,
social happiness are lacking.   One fact should receive
the earnest consideration, *primarily*, of all persons thinking of leaving home for India.   It is that the only

possible recompence for so leaving home is money. For
this they will have to give up almost everything which,
to the studious, makes life enjoyable. And they ought to
ascertain *definitely* what their prospect is, and put against
it what, as they will find a little farther on, is the life they
must expect. Now I am perfectly safe in saying that,
although not numerous, there are some young fellows
who are comparatively indifferent to money and wealth.
They are hard readers, never go to places of amusement,
are quiet and retiring, fond of the newspapers, and
always *au courant* as to the last thing in social meta-
physics, are admirably suited for office life, but unfortunately sometimes think town life is very irksome ;
that they would like to live in a little country cottage
"far from the maddening crowd," and grow roses and
strawberries in the day-time, and read books and
magazines at night. To such men (I have myself
known them) the life that they imagine prevails in the
tea districts seems to be just the very thing for them.
When they hear that it means isolation, they say with
a chuckle, "Just the very thing; I like being alone."
When ill-health is spoken of, they think they will
take exercise and live carefully, and so keep well ; and
they give up the substance of home peace, and a vocation for which they are admirably suited, for the
shadow of greater peace and greater quietude, and
then have to find out, with regret and sorrow that are
very sad to think of, that they are singularly well-
fitted for the quiet, studious regularity of home, and
singularly unfitted for the dreary, empty life of a

foreign land. They would willingly exchange their servants and their horses for the unpretending home of their sisters and brothers, and infinitely prefer the short ride every morning and evening by train or omnibus to " riding about all day in their shirt-sleeves, and never wearing a collar."

Now, on the other hand, there are many young men who are *not* of this quiet, studious inclination. They are fond of cricket, and riding, and football, and shooting, and rowing, and so on; and where the man previously depicted has, likely enough, never fired a gun in his life, our active friend will rise at any hour in the morning you choose to mention, and gladly go out fasting on the chance of finding rabbits to bang at in a turnip-field. Where the one glories in being alone in his sanctum with a scientific book and a good fire, the other delights in describing the figure of eight on the ice, or having, according to his idea, a jolly evening with a few friends. He is, more frequently than not, robust and ruddy, and likes to see the effect of telling the oftentimes slender reading man, as the latter shivers in the cold, that he bathes in cold water every morning of the year, and snow-balled his younger brother on the previous evening, as the only alternative of doing so to the passing policeman. He is full of animal spirits and bodily vigour, and is the kind of man who is well-suited for the tea districts.

The relative prospects of the capitalist and the mere appointment-seeker of course differ considerably. The modes of procedure for the former are varied. Moneyed partners for tea estates are sometimes looked for in England, and an opening made on the plantation for the investor; or the capitalist goes to Calcutta and effects the same thing there. While not for a moment insinuating that thus doing is risky, I think it far more satisfactory, and much more likely to prevent very probably eventual disputes, if a man will go to whatever tea district he may decide upon, and see things for himself. There will be no difficulty in doing this. Let him get an idea as to the neighbourhood of the district he fancies, and any firm in Calcutta interested in tea will direct him to the best agents for information as to that neighbourhood. He will then be able to write to planters who will be mentioned to him, and will not, I am sure, experience any difficulty. Let him state his business plainly—that he wants to look about for land to start a garden, or for a garden needing a moneyed partner, sleeping or otherwise; and any planter will do his best for such a man. Another plan would be to obtain a post (in London or in India) with or without a salary, as assistant on a factory to which he would proceed, and on which he would learn his work, looking about him in the meanwhile for an opening for his capital. I do not feel able to recommend one mode of procedure before another, feeling sure that circumstances will invariably determine the best way to work. A man might wish to invest in a new garden and to make it himself; and I would advise such an one to act as assistant for at least two years, in order to get an idea of his work. He will not have very much experience then, but sufficient to start with, if he has a few well-informed neighbours about him : at all events, he will have learnt the different modes of working with natives, contracts, &c. He need not think that this time will be lost to him, as he will be able to obtain in India good interest for his money while it lies unused, and will probably have made—or be able to make—a nice little profit on exchange.

I would advise no man to be in a hurry to decide upon his investment.   Many gardens, both old and new, at the present moment are greatly in need of financial help ; and while it may be said to be now a good time for investors, the rider must be added, " provided they are careful." The best thing for an intending share purchaser to do would be to obtain a report from an experienced planter, if possible, from another district, in which all points would be carefully considered and reported upon :—Tenure, buildings, labour, staff, machinery, communication, general plant ; ratio of increase in out-turn and expenditure during the last few years ; the exact state of the factory advance account ; the condition of the garden, as having been, or not, well pruned, drained, and carefully treated ; the number of hoeings in the previous year (to gauge the sufficiency of the labour) ; and, in addition, if possible, a report from London tea-brokers, as to the standing of the garden mark with buyers. I would not recommend any man to work as an assistant on the estate in which he has a share. The resident interest, unfortunately, generally results in dissensions between the

part-owner and the experienced manager ; and in·
variably the financially weaker one eventually goes to
the wall, and loses his post. Even should this not
occur, it is almost impossible for the manager not to
feel in some degree or other that his assistant is his
employer, and that virtually, although manager, he is
the subordinate Through this, the common interest is
likely to suffer. Or should a capitalist purchase a share
in a garden, and be working as assistant on a neighbouring one, he must not expect the manager of his own
(part) property to consider himself in any way under
the orders of his junior in experience. No agents would
exonerate a manager for so giving way. Sensible men
will, perhaps, say this is very needless advice. I thought
so myself at one time, but have since seen the need of
giving the caution. "Whom the cap fits," &c.

I had begun to refer to some estimates made a few
years ago, with the view of giving an idea as to the
cost of opening out land and making a garden ; but
remembering that each district has its peculiarities of
jungle, and of land measurements, and its own mode of
clearing and preparing land, I feel that it will be quite
useless to give, in a book that should be general, estimates that are applicable to one or two districts only.
In Assam, land is generally measured by the *poorah* —
equal to about an acre and a third ; in Cachar, the *hál*
(about five acres) rules ; and here also, contrary to
my Assam experience, a great deal of work is done
by contract with Bengali villagers —cutting thatch,
making bridges, nurseries, houses, &c. Then in some

districts even the jungle differs—heavy forest, grass, bamboo.

Although less varied, the value of planted land is still somewhat irregular. At one time there was a general rate of sale for tea in fee simple land (freehold), with a reasonable labour-staff, buildings, &c.

> Bearing-land over 5 years old, Rs. 800 to Rs. 1,000 per acre.
> ,, under 5 years old, Rs. 700 to Rs. 800 per acre.
> Non-bearing land 2 years old, Rs. 400 to Rs. 500 per acre.

But these rates have changed since I know of Rs. 1,300 per acre having been refused for above a thousand bearing acres four years ago ; but probably no such price would be obtainable now. Although in buying estates, good buildings are an inducement, they seldom count for much to the seller. Of late, some of the old concerns in the older districts have been offering parts of their originally enormous grants for sale. Land was taken up years ago by the thousand acres, seemingly to prevent another European opening out anywhere near ; but a good deal of this conservative spirit has passed out now, and the holders of old grants are glad to sell land that they cannot use. But land is obtainable from the Government on lease for thirty years at a total cost during that period of Rs. 2 per acre ; after which, I believe, the lease is renewed in perpetuity. (See Appendix.) But all timber on grants so applied for has to be measured and purchased. Taking up land on these terms is much easier in some districts than in others, the timber being the obstacle.

Even were I able (which I am not) to give the probable selling-price of land, bearing or otherwise, in all the tea districts of India, exceptions would be found to my figures, where owners of estates are very anxious to obtain additional capital. So having shown the intending investor how to obtain all necessary information, I must leave him to himself to do so. This, however, I will say to him in closing : that if he buy well and manage well, either personally or by deputy, provided his hopes for the future are moderate, he ought not to look forward to a residence of many years in India, unless he wishes to take a lump sum of money out of the country, or rushes into the everlasting new-clearance mania, referred to in another chapter. If he will be content with a remitted income, and satisfied with, say, 300 acres of plant, by putting in fifty acres per annum for six years, in nine years from starting he will have his acreage all bearing, and after staying through that year to enjoy one full manufacturing season from his property, he ought to be able to go home, provided he finds a good manager (as he would be easily able to). (See Appendix.)

Now for the case of the appointment-seeker. There are various conditions of engagement in England. Some of the Tea Companies with London Boards occasionally send to India young men introduced by Directors, shareholders, or others having influence with a Company's executive. There are many private owners, also, who appoint assistants in London. The terms of service vary much. Appointments may be given on three, four,

4

or five years' agreements, with or without a free passage ; or a man may be expected to pay his own expenses, and give his services gratuitously for twelve months.   Or it sometimes happens that, in addition to this, a premium is required, ranging from one to five hundred pounds.   Another plan is, for a shareholder in a private concern, resident in England, to arrange for a relative or friend to live on the estate in which he is interested, without a post, paying his quota of expenses to the manager, and looking out for an appointment. Or, as (unfortunately) frequently happens, young fellows obtain letters of introduction to mercantile firms in India who are interested in tea, and go out to them in the full expectation of having a post found for them.   I think I had better notice the last method first, and I am sure that Indian tea-agents will consider I am rendering a good service to their fraternity in discountenancing this mode of procedure in as strong a way as I can.   I know of one steamer that, amongst other passengers, in one voyage took out (I believe) fourteen young fellows with letters of introduction to the same firm in Calcutta, all of which asked the principals to find a post in tea for the writer's son, cousin, nephew, friend, or friend's friend, son, cousin, or acquaintance, and which had evidently been written in the belief that it was the easiest thing imaginable for posts so to be found.   As a member of the inundated firm remarked to me : " If such people would only write and inquire beforehand whether any chance of finding an opening existed, something definite might be arranged"; but as it is, young men generally get their outfit and take passage to Calcutta, each confidently believing his interest to be such, that, whatever may happen to others, he is sure to be given a post. Further, it often happens that appointment-seekers are in no way provided for an uncertain stay until, Micawber-wise, "something turns up." Even where a man is well provided with money, and willing to give his services gratuitously for perhaps twelve months, it is not as easy a matter as may be thought – as, indeed, I know is thought—to find an opening for an assistant. Generally in the tea districts, managers like to have their bungalows to themselves, and there is consequently the expense of putting up some kind of one for a new arrival ; in addition to which, some of the manager's time will necessarily have to be given to instruct the assistant in his work, help him with the language, &c. ; and the manager may have too much on his hands to be disposed for this. Young fellows who go out in the way described are often sent up to gardens where they have not been asked for and are not required ; and working without pay is, if anything, the reverse of an inducement to a manager to take an assistant, because it is liable to weaken the position that ought to be maintained between them. I would lay particular stress upon the great unwisdom of anyone going out thus, or, as it is generally called in India, "on spec." I know the London office of several amalgamated tea concerns in which a number of young fellows are working, and wisely waiting for vacancies to occur in India, instead of going out upon an uncertainty.

4 *

Should any relative or friend write and say, " Come out, and I will do what I can for you," that will be a different matter altogether ; but I leave the reader to imagine the private feelings of a Calcutta merchant who one fine morning is visited by fourteen young fellows, everyone of whom confidently expects an immediate appointment. I have spoken to such visitors, and have several times found them angry and disappointed because posts were not at once obtainable. I daresay they have a better knowledge of affairs now. Particularly at the present time it is a most unwise and foolish thing for anyone to go to Calcutta thus—on spec. Recent advices tell me that there is a large number of experienced planters in the city who have lost their posts on estates where bad times have compelled a reduction of establishment ; and many of them, being without resources, are glad enough to take posts upon the smallest salary that can well be offered Surely a novice going out with a whole bundle of introductory letters, cannot expect to be preferred to a man who understands his work, and is obtainable for a salary which in good times is given to new assistants. In the Appendix I give a list of the districts in which tea is cultivated, and also one of Calcutta agents, secretaries, owners, &c. If, through English influence, the reader can place himself in communication with any of these firms, he will be in the right road ; but I would most strenuously advise him, for his own sake, no matter what money he may have to keep him in India (unless he goes as a capitalist to invest), on no account to go out on spec.

I would here mention that some of the tea districts are at many days' distance by steamer from Calcutta, and the expense of reaching them is not inconsiderable.

While I readily admit that for some men who have so gone out posts have been provided, a large number of vacancies have been simply created because of insufficient funds to return to England ; and I also know of men who, being financially better off, have seen the advisability of returning, unpleasant and disappointing as was the proceeding. Indian towns are expensive places to live in ; and many of the vacancies that I have just said were created because men were in India, have since had to be closed, through tea prospects being too bad to support extensive establishments. But things once again are brightening. The London Directory contains a list of Indian tea companies ; and the industry, being now a very considerable one, has many representatives (socially) in England, who have interest or power to give appointments ; and I would recommend anyone desiring such to seek it in England, and not to go to India upon the merest chance of succeeding.

We will suppose that in one way or another the reader has secured an appointment, and gets ready for India. (He will obtain in the Appendix an idea as to what he will require.) There are several lines of steamers running to Bombay and Calcutta, and no difficulty will be experienced in finding a comfortable vessel. Regarding going away, I would say two things. The first is, that the festive family-gatherings and " farewell meetings " which generally take place when a

man is leaving home for the first time, frequently afterward cause more quiet sadness than pleasant recollection. I hope I am one of the last to say aught against
the love of kindred or family sentiment : but my own
experience has been that when the recollections of
" good-bye " gatherings come to mind, they carry a man
back over the ocean to his home with more distinctness
than almost any other recollection, and show to him
with an almost painful clearness that he is indeed far
away from his friends. I know that it is natural to
indulge in the demonstrative evidence of good nature;
but my advice is to keep it at the lowest measure
possible, because such outbursts of kindly feeling constantly arise in memory, and rather unsettle a man. It
is likely enough that when the subject of a farewell
meeting has been seven days out, and the vessel is
(possibly) running along the Mediterranean Sea, he will
think, " Ah! this time last week I had just left home
to go to Uncle Charlie's " ; and as the hours of the
night come in apace, the remembrance will perhaps
spring up of how, just about that time a week ago, he
kissed his little cousin in wishing her " good-bye," and
laughingly said he hoped she would not be too big for
the same thing when he returned. Ah! he feels considerably less jovial in thinking about it thus, than he
did in doing it. Return? It is a strange country to
which he is going, one of fevers, and cholera, and dire
sickness. Will he ever return? And he looks out into
the night, far across the ocean, and thinks of the
hundreds of miles a week has put between him and his

loved ones ; he wonders will they, just then, be thinking
of what was transpiring seven short days ago.   He
pictures faces becoming wrinkled, and hair growing
silvery, and thinks of hearts that have begun to yearn
for his return, even before he has reached his destination ; and it seems to him that he had better take a hand
at whist, put on a cigar, or play at draughts (solid ones)
with a passenger, in order to change the current of his
thoughts.   The future will have for the emigrant far
fewer rushes of recollection such as this, if there be but
a small number of monumental pillars in his memory's
citadel.   It may be almost said that the more joyous
such parting meetings are, the more unsettling will
their remembrance be.   Each man should strive to
leave England as soon after he has decided to go as
possible, and get away with as little social demonstration as may be ; for the less he has of this, the more
contentedly will he be able to meet the future with
whatever it may bring.   And let the evidence of affection
be great or small, the traveller will likely feel his going
away a great deal less than do those who remain.   The
glamour of excitement will be upon him ; and the bustle
of preparations, together with his roseate anticipations
of the future, will prevent him, until he has really left,
from realising the solid reality of his having done so—
that he is leaving home, and kith and kin, in the words
of the beautiful old song :—

      " It may be for years, or it may be for ever."

Ever ?   The only thought that has place in his mind

at the moment is that he is going away to make his fortune, and will return home in a few years, bronzed and (probably) bearded, and with plenty of money. I have no wish whatever to " pile on the agony "; but I write what has been the experience of many men in India, because I am anxious that young fellows should not spoil their lives by looking upon emigration as a continuous holiday, when really it is a most earnest and serious matter.

The other point is, to advise every man, to the best of his ability, resolutely to make up his mind to meet the circumstances of his life bravely, and, so far as he possibly can, to like his occupation—not merely to agree with himself to do so, but to actually *tell* himself that he will. Some persons may think this is altogether needless; I do not. It often happens that, perhaps years after a man has left home, he requires some mental stimulant to invigorate him, because he is much inclined to be disappointed with his position, with the country, and with nearly everything about him and connected with him. I have the testimony of several, that it will help a man much if he is able to remember that when arranging his cabin just after the vessel in which he left home cleared the docks, he told himself that he was going from home in the belief that he was acting wisely, and that he promised himself he would face the future courageously, and not be faint-hearted ; and the recollection of the past will very likely strengthen him, and he will resume his duties bravely.

We will take it, then, that our embryo planter is fairly on his way to India. While not wishing to draw a melancholy picture of the future, the outward voyage cannot be taken as a fair indication of the order of things before him. Oftentimes young fellows think, "Well, this is pleasant enough, and is only *on the way* to India ; what will the country itself be ? " I can promise that, in many respects, not quite so pleasant.

People leaving home for the first time, cannot be too careful on board the steamer. I am not going to draw up a moral code for the guidance of passengers, but would just say that India is a strange country, in which people know of each other, although living at distances, in a way which has no parallel in England. I imagine the cause to be, that as they go to the country in batches, everybody knows, at all events, a few persons in India ; and in speaking to locally-made acquaintances, it often happens that other passengers who are in remote parts are mentioned, and the listener seems to know them quite well. The incidents of a voyage belong and apply to passengers generally ; they are often retailed in different parts of the country, and most passengers are spoken of in such narrations, more or less, at some time or other. It is therefore advisable that each individual should be careful to prevent the voyage recording anything unpleasant against him ; for should he make an ass of himself in any way, it will be known in many parts of India. Oddly enough, it frequently happens that when such has been the case, a man does not hesitate to tell others of his own stupidity, yet thinks it exceedingly unkind of any other passenger to retail it of him. It is not an unusual thing in India, in holding a conversation after an introduction with a stranger, to be asked :

"By the way, didn't you come out from home in the *Magnet*?"

"Yes," you reply. "How did you know?"

"Oh! a friend of mine, Donison—a dressy little chap —has mentioned your name;" and then, *sotto voce*, "he told of how you were with him at Malta and lost your hat, when all of you had to get down the steps three at a time to the boats."

You do not feel obliged to Donison; if he made a fool of himself that is no reason why he should couple your name with his nonsense; but as voyage episodes are almost public property in India, if there is anything that can be said about you, you may pretty safely rely upon somebody telling it. "Prevention is better than cure": so the conclusion of the whole matter is, do nothing that you would dislike hearing of again; and if other people are less careful, then "do as you would be done by" regarding them.

Another piece of advice is, do not worry old Indians, because old Indians do not like being worried; and surely that is a valid reason for leaving them alone. If you see a portly old gentleman asleep on a deck chair, do not chalk at his feet in an outlined tablet "I am hungry"; also do not victimise any good-natured old person, who may have been kind enough to give you the Hindustani for a few words, by arousing him every morning for the translation of various useless phrases; because if you assail him thus, by rapping at his cabin door before he has risen, and inquiring, " If you please, Mr. Jellavey, will you excuse my troubling you, but I should be much obliged if you would be so good as to tell me the Hindustani word for ' pop-gun,' and the English for ' *mátwallah*,' which I heard a Lascar say as you passed by him last night," you are likely to receive the contents of his water-can over your head.*

I certainly do strongly recommend every passenger to acquire what knowledge he can of the language on his way out. As he will not be able to learn very much, if any, on the voyage, I would advise him to keep to Hindustani, which will help him (as a rule) in any part of Hindustan. But should he be able, he would do well so to learn from any passenger who has lived in the district to which he is going. Even (what passes for) Hindustani varies in the different parts of India; and many of the nouns and verbs used as Hindustani in Assam, have no place in what passes for that language in Cachar.

In novels of the startling order, there is often given a picture of the elderly Anglo-Indian, as a violent, ill-tempered, fire-eating individual, using all kinds of strong expressions, and even swearing in an unknown tongue. I can only say, for myself, that I have never met such a man. Social life amongst Europeans in India, no

---

* In reading this over, I am sorry to say that I feel it almost necessary to state that having myself seen these two modes of worrying perpetrated, I mention them in the light of censure, and not as an incentive ;—as was remarked by the Irish temperance advocate who gave each attendant at his lecture a glass of whiskey to prove what nasty stuff it was.

matter how rough the surroundings, aims always at the
maintenance of studied etiquette one to the other, in
both action and speech. Polished men leaving England
for India seldom, if ever, return to it rough and uncouth ;
indeed, results may almost be said to point the other
way. I was much surprised at not finding this loud-
speaking, arrogant, supercilious Anglo-Indian, of whom
I had read, and on inquiring as to his existence from
a quarter of a century resident in India, I was told
that he was imaginary. Certainly, my further experience at home—in business and at the Clubs—points
to the opposite of the picture drawn by (I suppose)
novelists who have never been in the country spoken of.
At the same time, having been, as a rule, accustomed
to social ease, Anglo-Indians, especially elderly ones,
have a strong aversion to being troubled. They are
willing enough to give you plenty of information about
India as experienced by themselves, but I would advise
inquiring minds to look to younger persons on board
for Lexical guidance.

It will be a wise thing to obtain a good map of India
before leaving England. It is possible to live in the
tea districts for years and to know scarcely anything
of other parts of the country. In returning home, most
people—speaking of India as they do of London—expect
you to know every place in it ; and it is easy enough
for a man to help himself much in this respect by having
a good map to refer to, after hearing places mentioned
in the course of conversation. (See Appendix.)

As to the voyage to India being pleasant or other-

wise, depends very much upon oneself. I shall pass
the subject now, leaving the passenger to ascertain for
himself the different places stopped at *en route*, the
various proceedings at Diamond Harbour and Aitchee-
pore, as he nears Calcutta, and suppose him arrived at
the City of Palaces.

He will have received—or should have obtained—full
information as what to do on arrival in Calcutta, to
whom or where to go, &c. Europeans in India are
very hospitable ; and a new arrival will find no difficulty
in ascertaining the way to set about his business. Office
hours may be said to begin from 10 A.M., and morning
calls are expected (if I remember correctly) between
12 and 2 o'clock. I think I had better, for a moment,
refer to the subject of a previous paragraph, and advise
strangers having social calls to make, to inquire of any
Calcutta folk on board what to say to the Durwán of the
houses they may call at, what that individual will say to
them, and so on. I remember a case of a newly-arrived
Doctor thus making a call, and who having learnt
the order of things, inquired of the Durwán, " *Mem-
sahib hai ?* " and receiving the answer, " *Hai,*" gave his
card, which was taken up-stairs. But when the door-
keeper returned with " *Mem-sahib Ap ko salaam det'ta,*"
Galen's disciple forgot the translation he had learnt, and
not understanding what the Durwán said, got into his
conveyance and went away ! For the benefit of the
uninitiated, I would say that the Durwán's observation
was, " The lady gives her salute (or compliments) to
you," which implies, " Please go to her." Should the

door-keeper when asked, "*Mem-sahib hai?*" reply
"*Mem-sahib nahin hai, likhin Missie-bábá-logue hai,*" the
visitor must act for himself; as I decline to be his guide
in such an event, and thus risk having this book eventually charged with bringing about what may be most
serious results.   This by the way; now to resume.

In all probability our tea-planter elect will not make
a long stay in Calcutta.   Of course, if joining tea estates
in Ceylon, he would have left at Colombo or Galle, or
if going to the Neilgherry hills, have probably disem-
barked at Madras.   He will easily obtain all information as to continuing his journey from the Calcutta
representatives of the concern he is to join, and we
will suppose that he makes a start and reaches his
destination.

And now, lest my own experience should mislead anyone as to districts I know nothing of, I will say that
the next part of this chapter refers only to Assam and
Cachar, although I have reason to believe (that with the
exception of the Darjeeling Terai) affairs are pretty
much the same, with possibly the advantage of less
unhealthiness and consequently less favourable climate
for tea.   And of these two districts, I believe I shall be
correct in saying that in Cachar planters are closer together, and have greater social advantages than Assam
ones generally have, as club-houses in the station, hockey-
clubs, &c.; and, I would just mention in passing, the
use of boats in moving about from place to place, more
than seems to be the case in Assam, or, at least, so far
as my own knowledge goes.   On the other hand, whereas

steamers reach the uppermost stations in Assam, on the Brahmapootra, all the year round, they can only go to Silchar (the principal station in Cachar) for about half the year, and country boats have to be used; and although local planters use them readily, the mode of travelling seems less pleasant to those used to Assam steamers.

It is usual, I believe, for young fellows looking to join tea properties, to expect that everything in connexion therewith will be very rough ; and because of this, many I know are surprised, on first arriving, to find much greater domestic ease than they anticipated. Certainly, there are frequent anomalies—or seemingly so—such as a moderately costly dinner-service and a fair display of plate on the table of a bungalow that has been made habitable without a pane of glass or a brick; or planters holding highly-paid positions wearing (to quote Josef Sprouts) white " trousers that are patched about like draught-boards, and boots that are fearfully and wonderfully made." But I think the new arrival will be most struck with the personal freedom that exists between managers and assistants. Particularly will this appear so to anyone who has left English mercantile life. Whilst it is advisable, and is, I should add, customary, for discipline to be maintained, it is done with an entire absence of that marked distinction which at home at once shows to the most casual observer which is the superior of two men in an office. This open demeanour is very pleasant; and although official squabbles do sometimes occur, the individual bearing of managers toward assistants, and

vice versâ, is one of thoroughly good-fellowship and freedom from restraint.   There are not too many of one's
own countrymen in the Indian tea districts ; and it seems
to be a mutually understood thing for those who are
there to stick together as much as possible.   Nothing
pleases natives so much as to see Sahibs at variance ; and
it is consequently the social duty of every man to guard
against gratifying the native populace in this regard.   I
may safely promise the new assistant that he will find
himself kindly received by all the men he may meet ;
and he will have more invitations to visit different
factories than it be wise for him to accept, at all events
at the first.

In beginning his work, I would recommend that the
young planter should resolve upon two things.   His
terms of service will give him a pretty accurate idea as
to his prospects ; let him study them carefully, and make
up his mind for a trip home in a certain number of years,
and work for this.   He will meet some men who have
been home after five years, and others who have been
out that time and are as far from being able to go home
as they were on first arriving.   The other thing is, to
use every effort to save, as soon as possible, sufficient
money to cover expenses home.   Cases happen sometimes of young fellows having to leave the country
through illness, after twelve months' stay ; and although
such cases are rare, they do occur.   When it is a matter
of life and death to get out of the country, and the
estate cannot pay for a passage home, and there is no
time to write to England for funds, nor any friends in

India from whom one likes to ask for temporary help, the position is a very unpleasant and critical one. A man never knows how soon he will be obliged to go home; but the future, as regards that event, will not trouble him at all if he have sufficient money banked to meet expenses. No one will blame a young fellow for saving money; it is the purpose for which nearly every European goes to India, and it is the last thing that many succeed in accomplishing. Generally, the really successful men are those who begin to save money when drawing small pay. It will help a man to effect this, if he will govern his expenses, as long as he can, by the English standard of value, *i.e.* that a rupee is (nominally) of the value of 2s., that 2s. is the tenth of a sovereign, and that a sovereign will take him more than a hundred miles from Calcutta towards home. The absence of shops and stores, excepting in a few localities, in the tea districts, generally compels men to obtain their requirements from Calcutta; and writing for goods is a pleasant occupation, and an easy means of obtaining them. What I might almost call the " Indian rule of dozens," is a great snare. It is not customary at home to buy toothbrushes, white waistcoats, trousers, and pipes by the dozen or half dozen; but it is in India, and the result is surprising. Indian prices, too, after English ones, seem more like those of fancy bazaars held in aid of chapel-building at home, than of genuine trade; but they are genuine enough, notwithstanding. Then as regards the tea districts, to goods thus priced there always has to be added the cost of transit.

It will be in every way desirable for the assistant to make himself familiar with the language, or languages, of his district, as quickly as possible. Let him stitch a few half-sheets of paper together, carry them in his pocket, and at one end write down all the words he hears and does not understand, and at the other everything he wishes to say and cannot; and then, when opportunity offers, ascertain what is necessary. He had better *write down* everything he wants to know, and not trust to his memory, or he will probably be asking the same question several times. If he has to look (as he probably will have) to his manager for guidance in this matter, I would recommend him to be regular in his time of questioning—say the first thing in the morning, or just before dinner in the evening, when the manager is not engaged with natives, or occupied with any work. Particularly let him be careful not to visit the bungalow just after breakfast, because he may find his superior just getting into a comfortable doze; and " I hope I am not disturbing you, but I have come to ask a few words," will likely enough cause the persecuted manager to think, " *Ap hum ko aisa dik det'ta roj bá roj.*" (By the time the assistant has troubled his manager a great deal, he will probably understand this sentence.) A source that often exists for obtaining information in the language, is the native doctor on the factory. These men are frequently able to speak a fair amount of English, but do not do so where the manager is a good linguist; or if they can speak only a little, they are likely to have dictionaries for reference. But the assistant must be careful to seek the Doctor Babu's help in this matter away from his house, as it is always an open question whether educated natives like an European to enter their dwelling. I would advise the assistant not to let his inquiring mind lead him into the error of continually pulling out his book under his manager's nose, should that (the manager, and not the nose) be the only source of information. Now and again will not matter, but regularly doing so will become something of a bore. If notes must be made out-of-doors, always endeavour to make them in the shade ; because the rays of the sun on anything white placed immediately beneath the eyes makes it almost blinding. Acquiring the language is an important matter. I believe I may say that assistants will find themselves thinking that when a native speaks English well, he must be a sharp fellow, and where, if at all, only badly, the reverse. Natives look on Europeans in a very similar light, believing that perfect speech represents long residence, and long residence a knowledge of their ways (literally, artifices) ; consequently, endeavouring to get the better of such a Sahib is useless. It may be somewhat hurtful to the feelings of new assistants to know that until they can make themselves understood, and thereby get work properly done, their salary is a loss to the factory ; so the sooner they overcome this, the better. Having gone through it all myself, I very readily admit the natural objection a young fellow feels to trying to speak when he is but too well aware of his ignorance, and thereby making, as he feels it, a fool of himself before natives. But he can only

5 *

learn the language by making mistakes and struggling on ; *and do this he absolutely must*, before he can be of any use. If he cannot *tell* people how to do a thing, let him *show* them; and if he is able to put a sentence together, with the exception of the verb (I am aware that the exception is important), let him substitute the English word for it, or say "hocus," or anything else, so as to complete his sentence, show what he wishes done, and then put down in his book the word he wants to know. Asiatics have a marvellous control over their countenances ; and it will be a really almost unpardonable error of speech that extracts a smile. And even should a young assistant be laughed at, he will have to bear it ; and, if wise, he will do so cheerfully, remembering that it rests with himself, and is dependent upon his own assiduity, to make natives appreciate him on the very ground they may at first laugh at him. I always found that bungalow servants and factory people of a higher status than coolies, at all times did their best to get at what it was intended by a new Sahib to convey; although, in afterwards remembering how I used to speak, it seemed that almost a process of mental surgery must have been necessary to arrive at my meaning. It is as likely as not that a man will sometimes feel dissatisfied—especially after being only a short time at work—and fear he is not making progress in the language. He need only look back and remember how much (or rather, how little) he knew on the first day of his arrival, to remove this fear.

As the planter settles down to his work, he will

probably begin to wonder what his prospects are for the more remote future. He will perhaps realise (in a way he has not previously) that in leaving home he has entered a course in which, for his own credit's sake, he ought to continue until he makes it a success. And the fact that men are near him who left home with precisely the same hope and intention, but who have up to that time failed, will make a new man particularly solicitous as to his own future. He will do well to start with the conviction that there will be no such thing for him as suddenly making a fortune. Tea estates do not contain diamond mines. In an earlier part of this chapter, I have shown that a capitalist, by planting fifty acres annually for six years, ought to be able to go home at the end of nine, the owner of a remunerative 300-acre garden. Perhaps I ought to have referred him to some instances in Cachar, where 400 acres were planted in three years, and even 800 acres in two years! These, however, were not the transactions of individuals, but of joint concerns or companies; and I advised for solitary investors. A new planter may think that if a capitalist must stay nine years in the country, what an awful time a man without money will have to wait! But this does not follow. Sometimes when a planter has brought his own garden of 200 or 300 acres into bearing, instead of going home he begins making another factory. Of course he can do as he likes with himself and his money; but I sketched the possible career of a man who would be satisfied with 300 acres, and make an estate of that area by degrees. This extent of land could be put under plant in one season ; but the cost of bringing it into bearing would be enormous. A new planter will notice that he does not come across many elderly men in the tea districts—or even middle-aged ones—and he will probably be told that Europeans cannot live to be old in the tea districts. Unpleasant truths of this kind will make him desirous of seeing how soon he can get out of the country. A future independence may be hoped for in several ways, and his own ideas as to affluence or comfort must guide the planter. He may look forward to putting by enough money from his salary in the course of a number of years to give him an income in England, or look to saving as much as will enable him to join two or three other planters in opening out a garden. More probably than not, he will change his way of thinking many times. He will differ from most youngsters I have met, if he does not, for some time after arrival, express his steadfast belief that he would not go home if he could. Indeed, the only exception I ever knew to this, was the case of a young fellow who was living in particularly comfortable quarters with a relative ! Very likely at one time our hopeful friend will make up his mind to save what money he can, join other planters in making a garden, remain on until it is brought into full bearing, and then go home, or sell out and go home, to make sure of his money. Or (probably after an initiatory attack of fever) he will decide to save £500 as soon as he can, and then go home. Later, in the cold weather, when he is feeling well and hearty, he will think that staying out until he is forty will not see him returning home for good at such a very advanced age, and so he will save his money to join other men in opening out, and not sell his share when the land comes into full bearing, but have occasional trips home, and so be able to wait until he can do so finally with a really good income. And then, perhaps on the following day, after he has quite determined on thus doing, he will receive long, loving letters from home, enclosing Christmas cards and telling of Christmas festivities; and as he sits by his fire in the evening, with the idea of his own garden running in his head, he will read his letters again, and thinking of the long interval between the then present and when this imaginary garden will be in full bearing and giving him a large income, be likely enough to say, " Well, I don't know—home is the best place after all; I think I should sell out when the garden came into bearing, and be content with the interest I could obtain on the money in England." Let me, in all kindness, tell these castle-builders, that they might as well write home to an architect to plan for them such a house as they would like to live in (as probably as not on the Indian bungalow style, only a great deal nicer, you know), as thus, years before they are ready, to plan their future for themselves. Their future is wisely hidden from them. But this I can say to cheer them, that the first 100 rupees they save is a good and sure foundation for the wheel of fortune to work on, if they will but continue steadily and perseveringly to add spoke to spoke

until the wheel is perfect. Also, that it will be early
enough to decide upon the use to which the money shall
be put, when it is obtained; and there will not be the
least difficulty in putting it into a garden or investment
of any kind fancied, at such a time. Indian rates of interest are generally higher than at home; but the great
cause of the financial disappointment of many men is
that they believed they could not begin to save when on
small pay, and they consequently have never saved at
all! I write thus, in the earnest hope that young
fellows will make an effort to begin to put money by, if
in any way possible, from their very first month's salary;
for in so doing they will be pushing forward the hand of
time on the dial of the future, as regards their going
home for good, and in thus making a beginning to save
will be practically guarding themselves against extravagance. When men have once left home, unless their
health completely gives way, they do not like to return
acknowledged failures. They say (perhaps) that "the
old people expected different things," and they will not
go home to disappoint them. Ah! the "old people"
would often have the absent ones back again on any
terms; and the knowledge of this only shows the failure
to be more complete, and renders the compulsory
sojourn more unbearable. Yet, I can see plainly enough
that the ability to go home as one would wish—as every
one anticipates in leaving—depends almost exclusively
upon oneself. But it will be a hard thing after years in
the country—years of health risked and strength lessened
—to have to acknowledge personal failure in this respect.

As time passes on, the planter will get into the steady swing of his work; an insight into the beauties of the native character, and the emptiness of his surroundings, will probably cause him to change his mind—or at all events to modify his notions—as to not going home if he could. And here I would say that tea-planters are undesirably placed in being surrounded by the lowest orders of natives. The writers on tea estates are invariably only villagers who have received a local education; and, as a rule, there is no higher native talent represented than that of the Doctor Babu. I mention this for tea-planters of all periods of experience, hoping it may somewhat reconcile them to their surroundings, and prevent them from basing their opinion of the entire native character exclusively upon the specimens at hand in the tea-districts. For in so doing, they judge unfairly men in other parts of India, of whose excellence they necessarily have scarcely any knowledge; and they also increase the unpleasantnesses of their own lives, by believing that they are living in a country that is almost as devoid of "really decent, reliable natives," as Sodom and Gomorrah in the old time were of righteous men. It is unjust to strike the intellectual average of any nation by the lowest of its peoples, and in the absence of its better classes. I mention this, because I have a long string of undesirables to show the intending planter, and I (wisely, I hope) begin by "pouring oil" into one of the many sore places in the lives of tea-planters.

This intellectually low condition of the cooly (I leave other people to write about the gentleman's morals) should cause consideration to be given to the fact, that while he undoubtedly possesses a head, the nature of its contents is still an unsettled question as regards brain. The homely Assamese express themselves innocently when promising to remember anything, by saying it shall remain in their stomach! But then, of course, the Assamese cannot strictly be called a learned people; and it is therefore quite possible that they do not know where their brains are (if they have any). Be this as it may (for I am sure I cannot decide the matter), coolies should not be expected to grasp the gist of an order directly it is spoken. It requires great patience to be thus forbearing, I well know; but when it is remembered that coolies are looked upon generally as the dubious possessors of brain power, they surely should not be hurried in their process of comprehending what is said to them. Young planters should hasten them judiciously, but never hurry them. It is possible to make one's life a constant jar and dissatisfaction, by allowing oneself to be worried and vexed unceasingly by the stupidity of coolies. Where any of them seem incapable of comprehension, the better way is to get a fellow cooly who is blessed with understanding, to interpret in his own way what is wanted, rather than to fidget one's existence by troubling over coolies' mental denseness. There are too many other things to make life the reverse of jovial, to render it wise to be vexed with coolies. Into these the planter will gradually be initiated as the time passes, and as he becomes accustomed to his work and his surroundings.

This will not take place, however, in the space of a few months. At least a twelvemonth will be necessary for the planter to see the complete routine of factory work, from pruning, seed-planting, and cold weather work generally, in one year, to the close of manufacturing, seed-gathering, &c. in the following. And although in the time mentioned, the assistant, in all probability, will have settled down to his work and be able to get along comfortably with the natives, he will not have become mentally acclimatised, even should he have done so physically, sufficiently to realise the life he has chosen. For even the changes of work on the factory will be novelties to him, as will the seasons, the native festivals, &c. And another one, of questionably pleasant character, will be in store for him in the tea-districts' mode of keeping Christmas. Nearly all Europeans spending Christmas for the first time on tea estates, think almost longingly of the home way of celebrating the great Christian festival. The climate will prevent all feeling of " old Father Christmas," with his snow-sprinkled beard and holly bough. As likely as not, assistants will be at work during part of the day, and will wonder at the indifference shown by longer-time residents to the festive occasion. By the time their second Christmas in India arrives, they will fully understand matters.

There will be very many things for the planter to become accustomed to—first of all, the heat. It is by no means a rare event for young fellows joining tea estates, to suffer from a great wish to become sunburnt, and to accomplish this they wear a small *topee* when they ought to wear a large one. I would first say that no one can be too particular in taking care of the head. I have known cases of very serious injury being done to the brain through youngsters thinking they could stand the heat, and thereupon wearing a hat giving but insufficient protection. In addition to the heat there will be the long hours and hard work—far longer and much harder than falls to men out of agricultural callings at home. If a new assistant be placed in the tea-house of a large factory, he must be prepared to exist in an almost parboiled condition for several months in the year. It was my own experience (and was that of others also) to be on duty in a tea-house—a brick building with a corrugated iron roof (which attracted and retained the heat beautifully)—and the heat of which may be possibly imagined when I say that the thermometer in the thatched, shady bungalow registered at times above 90° of temperature, and that in the tea-house there was a steam-engine to drive a rolling-machine, and for drying the tea fully 200 charcoal fires, which sometimes in the height of the manufacturing season were not out for days together. One does not know the amount of heat it is possible to bear, until it has to be borne. The style of dress adopted in jungle life assists in this matter immensely, as also does a quiet determination to bear the heat, and not to get irritable about it. Particularly does this apply in bed at night; and sleep being a most important agent in health, I think I am justified in mentioning it. My advice is, that on getting into bed, should the reader find the heat well-nigh overpowering—as he is absolutely certain sometimes to find it—he will do well to remember that he *must* bear it, and that restlessly throwing himself from one side to the other will certainly not make him cooler, and that the best thing to be done is to lie quietly without changing his position. It will also happen sometimes at night, often when a change is about to occur in the weather, that a man will wake up feeling parched and feverish, and almost gasping for breath; by taking at such times a copious drink of water, and quietly lying down again in bed, he will be almost sure soon after gradually to feel a gentle perspiration relieving the temperature of his body, and he will fall into a pleasant, refreshing sleep. It may almost be said that planters live in a state of chronic perspiration for eight months in the year, which becomes very wearisome towards the end, the more so as the rainy season is the unhealthy one also. I think I may safely advise every assistant going to the districts I have mentioned, calmly to make up his mind to be ill. Should he not have learnt the fact already, I would tell him that where tea thrives best, men die quickest. I take it on medical testimony that men must get ill sometimes in the tea districts. It is a thing common enough in England to find men in rude health, and who boast that they have taken no medicine for years. This kind of thing does not exist in the tea districts. Men have good health in the cold weather, but I may almost say never right throughout the rains. The planter who enjoyed the greatest immunity from sickness of all the men I knew in India, was very nearly a total abstainer, and took a glass of medicine every morning on leaving his bed. Fever and ague are the common foes to tea-planters, and are generally brought on by biliousness or by chills from getting wet. This reminds me of another frequent failing in the belief of new assistants—that they can get wet through with impunity. India is just the very last place where this can be done harmlessly. Wet clothes ought never to be kept on a minute longer than is unavoidable ; and the more closely this is acted upon the smaller will be the chance of fever. But in spite of all personal efforts, sickness is certain to attack, because of the malarious condition of the country. It is of no use thinking that careful living, exercise, and so on, will permanently ward off fever. I very readily admit that sickness is often brought on by carelessness when it could have been averted easily; but it will un-avoidably come at some time or other. Tea-district fever is particularly depressing in its effects, and one of the nastiest kinds of ailments that can be imagined. When an attack of ague has merged into fever, and the fever has passed off, there is an " all-gone " feeling that is quite indescribable. There is probably no pain (or if any, a head-ache), yet you feel completely unstrung. You wish to go out, yet want to stay in; you fancy some-thing to eat that you might possibly obtain in Calcutta (merely a few hundred miles off) ; you feel empty and hungry, yet have an aversion to eating; you do not like sitting down, yet know you are too weak to stand up long; if you want to read, your eyes wander over the paper; and then you want to sleep but cannot, or, perhaps, doing so eventually, you suddenly wake up to find a confederacy of mosquitoes thirsting for your gore and commencing operations on your nose, while their outpost guards almost make you use wicked swear-words, as they hum their infernal melodies into your unwilling ears. These are merely the *after effects*, when the trying part has left you. Such, indeed, was my experience; but, perhaps, the tormenting mosquito is less lively now; that is, if anyone has gained the reward offered some time since by a Calcutta paper to anyone who would advance a successful theory as to how to make out-door life attractive to the mosquito. Then, perhaps, when you fancy you are getting over the fever nicely, you will have a return of it, and go through all the same wretchedness again. An American journal, in describing the fever and ague of a malarious district, gives the testimony of a physician in New York city concerning it:—

" It comes creeping up a fellow's back like a ton of wild cats, goes crawling through his joints like iron spikes, and is followed by a fever which prevents the patient from thinking of anything save ' Greenland's icy mountains.' It isn't the now-and-again kind, but gets up with a fellow at daylight, and sleeps in the small of his back at night. His teeth feel about six inches long, his joints wobble like a loose waggon-wheel, and the shakes are so steady that he cannot hold a conversation except by putting in dashes. Then, perhaps, he gets better, and goes on making his fortune; then he gets worse, and goes on digging his grave; or, perhaps, he pulls through with only four diseases, no teeth, and a bald head, and returns to his native with a pile, and a disposition that only wants to be left alone. And his dear friends are very soon glad enough to leave him alone; for when they are drinking slings and cobblers, old Dollar Yellow-skin wants to sit by the fire; and when it is real cold and other people want a share of the warmth, old Shake-and-Rattle grumbles and wraps himself in blankets as hot as his hereafter, and thinks of the balmy days *when he only had the ague.*"

I should imagine that American malarious fever is of a more violent kind than the Indian; but the latter is bad enough, goodness knows!

In addition to this certain sickness, the long hours, the heat, and the really hard work unceasingly, there is a total absence of any social set-off against them. When work is done, as a rule (excepting in the cold weather), there is nothing to do save to have dinner and go to bed. The nature of the climate is exhausting, there is no one to speak to, the mosquitoes prevent your reading in peace, the night-air is unwholesome, and venturing out of doors is risky, so there is nothing to do but to turn under the mosquito curtain. Perhaps a little reading may be managed then, but more probably sleep intervenes. Then, after a night of uncertain rest, the bearer arouses the sleeper by bringing a cup of tea, and probably before 5 o'clock another day is begun. When a year has been passed through and the order of

garden work is known, there is very little variation in
the duties or in the life of the tea-planter. In all probability he made up his mind, in leaving home, to " rough
it "—believing that doing so meant living in a rough
house, devoid of any home comfort. But he will find
that, in the tea districts, " roughing it " generally
applies more to the mental than to the physical or
material side of life. A man may be by inclination a
veritable *bon vivant*, and yet settle down to a very plain
diet without often complaining. But the isolation and
dreariness that make up the life of the tea-planter, are
far harder to bear than the absence of the creature comforts to which he may have been accustomed. Planters
will get into the way of depending upon their work
exclusively for occupation day after day, and the result
will be that occasionally they will wake up, as it were,
to the mental barrenness of their lives, and feel that
they are living an unvarying existence rather than a pro-
gressive one—a life in which the work of each day will
be monotonously like that of the preceding one, and the
work of each year just the same as in the one that has
passed. *Redit labor actus in orbem.* Men will become
excellent tea-planters, but otherwise be rusting in knowledge. In brief glimpses at English papers, they will
see the introduction of new theories into social meta-
physics, new agents in domestic economy, and new
organisations of the economy of politics ; but all these
things will be far removed from life in the tea districts.
Leisure will be passed in the superficial reading of a
Calcutta daily paper, perhaps a little gardening, possibly

a small amount of botanical application and attention to
the indigenous *flora* around one, occasional strolls with
a gun, or rides on an elephant, on the chance of a little
sport, and so on, year after year ; the planter perhaps
saving money as a recompence for his curtailed happiness, or perhaps not. There will be times when, glancing
at the paper in bed, something will set his mind on
home; or perhaps his English letters will do so ; and
he will wonder to himself how it is that the glitter that
surrounded Indian life, while he was yet in England,
has so completely worn off. He will think of his
friends, who are marrying and advancing in life, and
ably filling social positions which have no parallel in
the Indian tea districts. He will look the future in
the face ; and thinking that until he is able to go home
his life will go on in the uneventful lines that have
now become so familiar to him, will almost envy people
who leave England for America or the Colonies, where
they find a white population and English institutions.
But, fortunately, the gong on the following morning,
will put all such thoughts as these out of his head, if
he be a sensible man. Perhaps it may happen that he
spends a night with a friend; and if the two are nearly
of an age and have been in the country about the same
time, in staying up after dinner to chat as is customary
when one is not alone (particularly if the day be Sunday),
they will very likely begin to talk about Sunday at
home, give some of their recollections of certain Sab-
baths, and gradually glide into talking of the present
order of things, and comparing it with that of the past.

And possibly—as I have known it to be—the conversation turns on churches and chapels; anecdotes are told respecting them, and by degrees favourite chants and tunes are hummed, and perhaps at last even part of the evening Church service, or a hymn is sung through. And the feeling that accompanies this retrospect of the blessings of home, differs vastly from that which some time before had led to the observation, "I wouldn't go home if I could." Very strange do these recollections make one feel on saying "good night" to one's friend, and turning into bed. Young fellows at such times are only absent sons and brothers; they are Indian tea-planters when they begin work next morning. The opinion of one planter at such times as these, I know to have been that when the anticipated glitter and glamour of the residence in India had quite worn off, there was absolutely no real recompence whatever for leaving home; a "free and easy life," or even money banked, notwithstanding.

I write thus, so that young fellows who want to go to India may examine themselves and see whether they are strong and determined enough, not in body merely, but in the under-currents of their nature, to exchange home for a salary, and to live a life in which there can be no home, as English people interpret the word. The quiet talks of the old country as given above, I admit, are very rare, and occur generally when young fellows have been out not more than two or three years. Likely enough the same men afterwards meet frequently, without again getting into the same channel of conversation. Then

6 *

there are many men—well suited to be tea-planters
—who, I believe, do never think or feel in the way described.   I have said that these unpleasant retrospective
views generally occur only after a short residence in
India.   Men who regret leaving home see that they
have entered upon an unsatisfactory course, and must
pursue it, there being no other course open.   They
accordingly cover up the past.   What is it that George
Eliot says, with such wonderful truth, regarding the
sudden ending of a joyous anticipation ?   " Hope closed
its wings, and became remorse."   But while some men
bury the past because thinking of it is useless, others
adopt the opposite extreme, which is equally undesirable
—they occupy the present in anticipating the future,
when they will be at home.   I believe thinking sometimes of returning home does a man good ; but thinking
of little else is very harmful ; and as it necessarily
takes away energy that should be given to work, virtually results in a moral breach of contract, inasmuch
as undivided attention is not given to employers' interests.   At the same time, these day-dreaming assistants
would not like to be told they are breaking faith—possibly they do not know it.   These are the men whom, in
previous pages, I particularly cautioned against going
to India—quiet, reading men who are fond of home,
and averse to out-door occupations.   They are occasionally to be found on tea estates, and constitute the
greatest trouble a manager can have.   They are far
worse than   uncertain-tempered assistants, who can
work, but will not ; for these unsuitable individuals

are most anxious to work, but cannot; they may
have capital abilities, but are unable to apply them
to tea-planting. Managers talk kindly to them, write
stern official letters, "good fellow" them, and threaten
to report alternately, but it is of no use; the assistant is as anxious to give satisfaction as the manager
is willing to be easily satisfied, and yet the work is
not done. The assistant tells himself that it is an
extraordinary thing—he knows he has a pretty clear
idea of his duties, but sees no beauty in them; the
manager knows well enough that the assistant understands his work, but does not do it, although at all times he
is professedly most anxious to do so. The cause is very
simple—total unfitness. A man who is well suited for
writing letters and posting ledgers, is generally altogether
out of his element in standing over gangs of coolies
hoeing ground day after day, and month after month.
He is really anxious to understand his work, but as soon
as this is accomplished he tires of it; *he lacks application
for the work which is foreign to his capacity.* As he walks
amongst natives hoeing, he is likely enough thinking of
things or people in England; and the coolies may slash
right into the lateral roots of the bushes, and actually
not be noticed.

When the novelty of their work has passed by,
men who thus join tea estates occupy their time
by planning for the future, and are of scarcely any
use in the present. I have seen them—young fellows
who are uncommonly brisk, when (presumably) supervising coolies, in getting on to the road if they see

a Sahib approaching, so as to have a chat—who often enough have the theory of tea-planting at their fingers' ends, are fairly good linguists, and so on, but who are no more fitted to be tea-planters than they are to be soldiers, and who will never be practical planters, let their stay in India be as long as it may. They dream away their time out of doors, and plan it away indoors; suffer from frequent attacks of *ennui*—or what would, perhaps, be better described by the well-nigh obsolete Saxon word " wanhope"—and virtually lose the present in anticipating the future—anticipating it in a way that will never be realised, because life is earnest and real, and has no prizes for dreamers.

At the same time, practical men will find many opportunities for escaping from mental stagnation and profitless despondency in the acquisition of amusing, edifying, or valuable knowledge. Very much that is interesting and instructive is to be learnt regarding the respective customs, religions, castes, legends, and proverbs of the Hindus and Mahommedans, together with something of their national history. A knowledge of these matters would often tend to the better management of coolies, would occupy the planter's thoughts, which are too often solely upon work, and enable him, when visiting home, to give people some ideas for which they always look, and of which they generally have some knowledge, as to the inner life of natives, and the vast difference between the two great factions. Then, perhaps, when planters come home, they will like the writer rush into print with what they have learned in India.

The redeeming feature of life in Assam and Cachar is the cold weather, which is thoroughly enjoyable. The days generally are bright and fairly warm, but the nights and mornings are chilly, fires are going in the bungalows, warm clothes are brought out of seclusion, mosquitoes go to Calcutta, work begins later and ends earlier, blankets are wanted on the beds, and dinner is served sooner to give a good long evening. And whereas in the rains the dinner-table is occupied by a thousand and one gems, in the shape of all the flying insects which are peculiar to "India's coral strand," and which are attracted by the lamps, in the cold weather one is able to see the design of the damask, and the soup is not a joint-stock concern, in which locusts and Norfolk Howards, and aerially-inclined beetles of a sable hue, have the chief interest. Shooting-parties are sometimes organised, and a few days of camping done ; or card-parties are arranged for friendly games, where planters live near together. Work is much more varied than in the rains, gardens are pruned, and, of course, manufacturing ceases ; horses are rested, as walking is delightful ; English vegetables are planted and brought to perfection ; and planters sit down to breakfast and dinner, after walking all the morning or afternoon, with a great appetite for solid food, and not exactly an aversion to the regular quantum of Bass's tincture. Men pull themselves together in health and spirits, and the cosy evenings seem more like home than in the trying months of the rainy season. Good health makes men cheerful, and when men are cheerful they are generally hopeful, and when men are hopeful, no country can be altogether bad, but must certainly suit some of them—as, indeed, it may safely be said, the tea districts, taken altogether, do well suit many men.

———————

CHAPTER V.

THE PLANTER ON LEAVE.

AFTER the many unpleasantnesses and vicissitudes here recorded, the planter, possessed of hard-earned savings, and probably of the too easily obtained fever, ague, spleen, or liver complaint, finds himself at his leave-time. In Assam, he hies to the nearest steamer station, and takes the first vessel for Goalundo; in Cachar, he probably hires a "green" or a country boat, lays in a stock of provisions and tobacco, and makes a start for the same place. The enjoyment of his rest can only be understood by those who work as hard as tea-planters have to work, year after year. Our traveller on the Assam steamer probably meets a few other planters also going home, together with one or two going to Calcutta for a change, and also, even more probably, with several taking a short river-trip to recover from the after-effects of a bad go of fever. How pleasant is life to the traveller on the Brahmapootra steamers! how very enjoyable to a man who has been

hard at work for years, and is now resting on his homeward way ! The *cuisine* is far superior to anything he
has had in his jungly quarters, and he can obtain tonic
and soda-waters. Instead of passing weeks together in
the company of himself, he has pleasant intercourse
all day long with planters from different parts of the
province ; and, if he be sick, as he is exceedingly
likely to be if going home, he will, as a general rule,
have, as the writer had, every possible care and attention, and almost womanly sympathy, from the skipper
of the steamer. There is not much to do, except to kill
time ; no young fellows to chat with about the outward
trip, as is often the case in going up the river ; so the
time passes in *gapping* with passengers from other parts
of the province, and hearing of men met long times
before. It is surprising how tea-planters who have once
met remain *au courant* as to each other's movements
through a long period of time in which they do not
meet.

So the steamer trip passes pleasantly. The planter
will have seen too much of village life to care to run
ashore at the different stations, excepting, possibly,
when one is reached at sunset, and then a short stroll
is taken " *Háwá khan'na ko.*" Very possibly some
delay occurs at Serajganj and Kalliganj ; and the
difficulty of waiting patiently while an unlimited quantity
of jute is shipped, can best be understood by those who,
after years of absence, are returning home, and thus find
themselves delayed by a mass of produce, which lacks
even the interest of estate marks, as in the case of tea.

But eventually Goalundo is reached, and baggage is removed to the station. How very strange it seems to the planter to be thus in civilisation again, after a long residence in the upper wilderness! How the whistles of the engines jar upon his sense of hearing, and yet seem almost melodious in the knowledge they impart of the entrance to civilised life, and the "way home!" One's voice sounds almost strange in asking for a railway ticket, and one certainly feels strange in the moving of a railway train—at least, such was the experience of the writer. For years past all locomotion would have been under the planter's own governance—horse, elephant, boat, or buggy—and progress or stoppage in his own hands, and his safety dependent upon himself. But now, as the engine puffs, and the whistle screams, he feels himself being carried away irresistibly, and there is almost a slight feeling of uneasiness at his inability to control his own movements. The Sealdah station is reached at length, and a *gharry* taken to probably the Great Eastern Hotel. Here, even more than at Goalundo, the re-entrance into civilisation is striking. Of late years all the animation about him would have been the outcome of the planter's own orders. He has known what ought to be the work of almost every man he has met, and he has been treated with consideration and respect. But here, in the (so-called) City of Palaces, to begin with, no one presumably knows him, no one cares who he is, and people pass him in total indifference. To express matters mildly, the planter feels strange. It may perhaps be remarked that he will possibly likewise feel strange, when he finds himself sitting in one of the cool refreshment-rooms of the Great Eastern Hotel, drinking iced—well, Soda-water, or eating an ice for the first time for years. (Very likely he remembers that on arriving in Calcutta before, he had not ordered iced Soda-water.) There are very few tea-planters who have anything but kind words to say of Calcutta.

Our newly-arrived planter makes his way to the office of his garden agents, by whom he is sure to be received most kindly, and from whom all information as to London steamers, &c. can be obtained. I think I had better pass through this stay in Calcutta; it is generally a whirl of excitement—buying things, dining with friends, going to the steamers, and so on—writing letters or reading books being irritating in the monotony of the exercise involved.

At length the steamer chosen makes a start, and after passing through the broad expanse of the river Hooghly, gets out to sea. Ah! the glorious, bright, blue, water! How often, when tossing on his bed in the furnace of fever, has the remembrance of the outward trip returned to an invalid's imagination; and more lately, in his convalescence, he has felt that all he needed to give him a full return of strength was a good blow on the ocean. And now, when he is again on the sea, how exhilarating is the effect. He forgets to remember the unpleasantnesses of jungle life; in the first rush of joyous realisation he thinks of nothing but the pleasant fact that there he is at last, with his back to India and his face toward home; that he is inhaling ozone which will build up a new man in him, and give an appetite that will make quinine insignificant. But as it is desirable that this description should be as exact as possible, it may be well to leave the planter here for a short season : because it is not unlikely, that by the time he has fully realised the beauties of the far-stretching ocean, he may consider it a discreet act to investigate the beauties of his cabin ; and prompted by unspoken intimation of internal disquietude, he retires thereto, to meet, as calmly as may be, the preliminary demonstration of preparation for acquiring the good appetite before mentioned. Or, in plainer parlance, he goes to his berth, the victim of an irresistible inclination to throw himself away.

We will now suppose that he has conquered this temporary indisposition, and is beginning to feel a new man. How enjoyable the sea voyage is ! Pleasant society, good food and a relish for it, no anxiety, no work, very possibly musical evenings, and, better than all things else, the knowledge that he is on his homeward way— these things will tend to make the voyage indescribably delightful to the planter. Particularly will the evenings be pleasant, quiet, and delicious, and without mosquitoes. It will surely be going not wide of the mark to say that in some of these periods the planter will sit on deck in a long cane chair, and indulge in a reverie and a communion with himself. He will think of the home to which he is returning, and how he left it—a lad, perhaps, with (what have since proved to have been) extravagant notions as to the glory of life in India; returning home after years of rough isolation, of con-

stant peril to health and life, years in which he has lived
a life wild in its surroundings and lonely to himself—
returning to a home, which by reason of long absence
and an intimacy of correspondence only, has become
almost a myth to him.   And he will think of those good
fellows, his brother planters, still on their estates, trying
to sleep in the oppressive atmosphere, and worried by
mosquitoes ; of the possible amount of tea made to date,
and as to how his successor is getting on, and treating
certain sections of the garden, regarding which particular
advice was given.   He will think very likely of the
manhood that has come to him in his years of absence,
of how parents, and brothers, and sisters are counting
the days to his expected arrival ; and without saying so,
he tells himself that fever and ague, and curry, and rice,
and coolies, and estimates, and jungly *burra-hhannahs*,
and mosquitoes, and *bádját syces*, are abandoned for a
time, and that after hearing from it, and writing to it,
and thinking and dreaming about it for years, he is
returning home.   And, unless my conception of human
nature is very erroneous, there will come into a man's
heart—no matter how little he may have thought on the
subject in bygone years —a feeling of exultation that he
has not left his bones in India, and a keener, deeper one
of thankfulness, that his life has been spared.   It is of
no use to jeer at the fever of the tea districts ; and,
strange to say, least of all may strong men despise it ;
therefore continued preservation from its fatality gives to
all men a cause for gratitude and thankfulness.   Perhaps
to some who have knocked about the world, and finally

wound up in India, this may seem an overdrawn picture ;
but it is a true one as regards those who only left home
to go to India and have not travelled elsewhere.   There
is a soft place in the heart of every man for his nativity ;
and harsh and rough, and lacking all social and domestic
softness and gentleness as a planter's life invariably does,
there is sure to come to him on this, his homeward
way, a recollection of what his home and kindred were,
the knowledge of what he is, and a speculation as to
what those he left behind him will prove to be.

Returning home!   The process of returning is pleasant enough, but what is his reception on reaching his
destination ?   Something far surpassing all that was
imagined !   The planter's position on his factory as
Burra Sahib will have been insignificant as compared
with what he will be considered in his own family-circle.
Everyone will suppose that, coming from India, he has
plenty of money ; everyone will ask, even in the hottest
days, whether " India isn't ever so much hotter than
this ? " and the need of maintaining the lionism of the
moment as a marvel and a salamander, will suggest his
answer without my giving it here.   But I may as well
say plainly, that some of the English summer days will
try the planter more than regular roasters in the Assam
rainy season.   The cause is the clothing.   I might
follow up the inquiries of the London press, and ask
how is it that English people will persist in retaining
here the very worst kind of dress for hot weather.   The
planter at home will feel the heat most in his head,
at his neck, and in the small of his back ; and I

really believe I may say that in these places he will feel the action of the sun more acutely than persons who have never left England. He will have been used to riding in India, but at home will do a much larger amount of walking than he has been accustomed to; his bodily temperature will be increased thereby, and he will feel it more than do permanent residents. Yet the English summer heat does not continue as does that of India. There may be hot weather for a few days, but not for seven or eight months; neither are there the awful nights of the Bengal tea districts, which, by their heavy atmosphere, are far worse to bear than the days. Three or four hot days in England generally result in a thunderstorm, which cools everything for a time. The planter home on leave will need to be careful of himself. He can stand a fair spell of hot weather, but the sudden fall of temperature common in England will try him sorely. A hot day is frequently followed by a positively chilly night, and an Anglo-Indian is liable easily to catch a bad cold in the hottest summer weather.

In most respects, England is very enjoyable to the planter on reaching home at first. Reunion with his relatives, of course, is pleasant beyond description. Then it seems, particularly in London, that surprising value can be obtained for money, compared with Indian rates, and numerous things that are of no use are consequently bought, because they are cheap. But there is a questionably pleasant side to English life. The planter misses his bearer, for one thing; and great as is supposed to be the bane of European life in India on the score of servants, in many respects Anglo-Indians would prefer the Eastern order of things to that of home. The amount of dressing which is necessary, although perfectly reasonable, is irksome to a man who has been used for years to dress strictly for comfort; and kid gloves become invalided with amazing rapidity on the hands of a *jungly-wallah*. There are many things, too, beyond personal likes, which are not palatable to persons from India. It seems strange to be waited on by people of one's own colour; and the scenes of street-rowdyism, the wholesale massacre of the Queen's English, the unmistakable evidence of terrible poverty in some districts, and, not least of all, the objectionable attendance of the street vendors of various articles—all these things will be very unsightly to the planter, and almost painful in the misery they indicate. Nothing of the kind has met his sight for years; everyone of his own colour has been looked up to, and to the general (native) public there has been no sign of distressing poverty, even on the part of the lowest-paid assistants. It will be an odd thing if our planter is not appealed to for testimony of the awful depravity of the mild Hindoo, and the success of missionary work; but it will be even more odd if, to the manifest disappointment of his inquirers, he does not unhesitatingly express his belief that charity ought to begin at home, and his conviction that he has never witnessed such scenes of helpless, ground-down, awful poverty, even in the Indian bazaars, as he does amongst his own countrymen in the metropolis of the world. When the single fact of being white

7

has for years been a sufficient introduction to the home of any planter, it will be with a feeling of a keener edge than dislike that evidences of social misery are seen. People who have never been out of England talk about the *prestige* of the white man ; but I think the peculiarities of life in the tea districts enable planters to speak upon this subject with much deeper feeling. The scenes are so common to the resident Englishman that they are passed almost unnoticed; but they jar most unpleasantly and painfully upon a man who has been absent for years, and who has seen no indication of want on the part of his countrymen.

There will be found changes in one's home-circle on reaching England that will make the planter ask himself whether he did wisely in selecting India as the field of his labour. Very likely he will have remembered his younger brothers as little fellows only, all through his absence : he will reach home to find them grown up and holding definite social positions. Many of his former friends he will find married, and having homes that will make him think rather unkindly about his *cutchá* erection of sixty feet by forty, built east and west. He will find his brothers and friends ahead of him in many things ; possibly students of various scientific subjects in their leisure time, members of literary associations and discussion classes, and, in their own circles, prominent characters. Into such intellectual cliques, it may be almost safely asserted, the planter will not feel himself qualified to enter. He can speak fluently one or two Indian languages, he thoroughly understands the culture

and manufacture of tea, has a slight knowledge of agricultural chemistry, can ride well, is ingenious at pic-nic
parties, is open-handed and open-hearted, and has
money put by ; but his life for several years has led him
far from scientific or generally intellectual channels, and
he has had no time for studying matters not connected
with tea. He can make good roads in jungly wastes,
but has not learnt much geology in the tea districts.
He can give you a fairly accurate delineation of the
Hindoo or Mahomedan character, but not in phreno-
logical phraseology ; and he can make large substantial
bridges, but very likely does not know the respective
specific gravities of wood and iron. No ; his life is
necessarily practical rather than theoretical. He can
give a reason for doing whatever he does on his factory,
but for the thoughtful study of subjects not germane to
tea he has had no time.

But whilst many of the social phases of English life
may seem very desirable—as indeed they are—and whilst
also, they may make the planter think his jungle life to
be sadly wanting in social and intellectual advancement,
he will be almost sure to think that in the matter of
occupation he has decidedly the advantage of men in
England who are not their own masters, and even of
many who are. However willing he may be to uphold
the maxim " *Labor ipse voluptas*," it will be difficult
sometimes not to think that in England, compared with
the custom in the Indian tea districts, it is very servile.
He will find that many years of service with a firm give
an *employé*, in most cases, no license as to attendance ;

7 *

and wet or fine, in summer or winter, 9.30 or
10 o'clock A.M. has to see even a highly-paid assistant
either at his post or failing in his duty. In itself there
is, of course, nothing far-fetched in this; only it is so
entirely different from the order of things which obtains
in a planter's life. Taking work for work, the Indian
hours are far longer, and the work much harder, than in
England; but in the former case even the youngest assistant is not bound to his work by a few minutes. Besides
which, notwithstanding the many social advantages and
the comforts of life in England, it will need but little per-
ception to see that where there is an absence of capital
or influential friends, a young man in England is likely
to be the servant of others all his life through. In the
Government service, of course, he may look to receive a
pension after many years of work ; but in commercial
centres, and in London business generally, whilst he has
a chance of an eventual partnership, he has a far
greater one of being a servant always. He may be able
to save and invest money advantageously, and thereby
obtain an independency ; or he may save money as long
as he earns it, and even then not have saved much at
the end. I think there can be no doubt that where
two young fellows start on an equality, one in England
and the other in the Indian tea districts, given that they
are of an equal mental calibre, and neither possessed of
money or influence, that the Indian one stands an infinitely better chance of success, in a greater measure and
at an earlier date, than the one who remains in England.
But then he takes the chance at the risk of his life, or

of the possibly permanent detriment of his health should his life be spared; and he accepts the prospect—or, I should say, the certainty—of years of an undesirable life, in the hope that the after ones may prove them to have been worth the sacrifice. It is altogether impossible to say which of the two is the wiser. If the Indian one comes home with a good income, the remaining one —not knowing the kind of life the other has had to put up with for years—may think he is the worst off, working still, and in all probability being likely to work, until he can no longer do so. But there would have been times when the now successful planter would have thought of and envied the home-peace in a healthy climate enjoyed by the other—home-peace and health, for which money and success seemed no recompence. And thus the matter stands: neither case can be pronounced the best or worst.

I have mentioned the signs of individual poverty, which at first will seem strange and unpleasant. Let me not forget the converse. The evidences of wealth— and the social status which invariably results therefrom —will act stimulatively on the planter, and make him hopeful for the future. He will probably meet men who have made Indian residence pay, and others who have made tea pay; and he will be willing to work on, striving and hoping for a like result to his labour. I have elsewhere shown the chance he has of making a position for himself. The trip to England, provided he recovers, or is in good health, on the working side of the question, causes him to prefer his Indian life to that led by men in England. And after some months of rest, he begins to wish to be back again. His life has been a very active one, and masterly inactivity does not suit him ; and the activity consequent upon visiting friends, exhibitions, and museums, is not congenial to him after a few months. He has probably become tired of hansom cabs, and wants his horse as a regular sequel to breakfast. He has begun to question the one-sided pleasure of spending money and earning none, and so resolves to get into harness again. Putting from his mind—as far as is possible—the parting " good-bye " which he knows must come, he tells himself that the sooner he recommences to nourish his system largely upon curry and rice, the better for him (financially). So he lays in an outfit which is useful, and not largely ornamental, as was probably the case when he left home before, takes his passage on a steamer possessing comforts which ocean-travelling has taught him are desirable, gets through the " good-bye " from home, and turns his face again toward India, mentally and physically able and willing once more to take up the lesson of life, vigorously and cheerfully.

CHAPTER VI.

THE FINANCIAL ASPECT OF PRODUCTION AND DISPOSAL.

THE present position of the tea industry is such as to lead me to hope that the following observations may be of some use. I was almost tempted to head this chapter " *De Omnibus rebus,*" as correctly indicating it, but thought the heading given would, while being applicable, receive more attention. If the remarks seem somewhat disjointed, I would say that the number of points to be noticed renders this almost unavoidable.

Representatives of several old concerns have of late been expressing themselves as very anxious at the falling off in price and quality of their teas ; and the professional reply given to comfort them has been that their teas are quite as good as those of other concerns with which they have ranked for years. This, it is needless to say, is perfectly correct ; but the fact that one weakening article is not weaker than others in a similar plight is no explanation of the mischief, nor a particularly satisfactory solution of the unpleasant state of affairs. There can be no doubt that, of the concerns which stood highest in the market some years ago, several have fallen altogether into the background, and comparatively new marks have taken the lead in high prices. There has been found to be deterioration in strength and flavour in the teas of favourite marks, and the matter is undoubtedly a very serious one. I shall be inviting a torrent of disclaimers from some quarters, when I say that this falling off is caused by the gradual exhaustion of the soil, which has been steadily drawn upon for years without any recuperative aid being given in manure, or in dressing of any kind. Writing on the subject of manure in *Tea in Assam*, I expressed my belief that high cultivation of good soil rendered manure unnecessary, even if not undesirable. The *Indian Tea Gazette*, in reviewing my work, disagreed with me altogether on this point. I myself think differently now on the subject from what I did when previously writing; yet I would say that my then way of thinking was the result of my training, and my belief the very general one held in Assam. Further experience in India, however, and the most manifest deterioration in quality of well-known teas offered for sale in London, have led me to submit this question to two different scientific agriculturists—one of the Cirencester College—and the result of my representation seems to me to be so important, that I risk the wholesale disagreement which will ensue, by stating plainly what I am told must be the sequel. There is really no cause whatever for surprise that old gardens should be sending home inferior teas, seeing that some of them have been drawing on the soil for more than a quarter of a century without ever returning any nourishment to it, excepting a few scattered prunings, year after year. Tea-growing at the best may be said to be a system of scourging crops, which is quite contrary to the principles of good agriculture. It is not to be expected that even the most fertile land can continue, unaided, to give sustenance to vigorous bushes from which leaf is plucked for eight months annually, and in such a way as to bring out more leaf and draw more plant-food from the soil. Cultivated land in England is relieved by a variety of crops, each of which to a certain extent rests the soil as far as can be, in respect to the properties drawn upon by the previous one. This system of rotation crops is followed out as much as possible; although perhaps some farmers have but a vague notion of the principle while carrying out the practice. There is no relief of this kind for tea-land. Year after year the fertility has been taxed, and now the owners are beginning to be troubled by the discovery that the produce is weaker and of less value, that the reputation of their teas is falling in the market, and that other concerns of a comparatively recent existence are coming into notice. No wonder! It would be an odd thing indeed if land could for ever go on producing valuable tea. Produce tea it might, just as it would grass and jungle, and as neglected fruit-trees produce fruit—but which is hardly worth eating—and the leaf coming from impoverished land, while being undoubtedly tea, would lack the

essential qualities to make it marketable. The more carefully the matter is thought upon, the more extraordinary
it seems that planters and owners should have gone on
all this time in the apparent belief that the soil would
never become bankrupt. More particularly does this
apply to Assam, where oftentimes men appear to be
quite aggrieved if the possibility of the soil becoming
impoverished is mooted. "Oh, no ! They manure in
Chittagong and the Kangra Valley, and other districts,
where the soil is poorer—we do not require it in
Assam."   Just so ; and the obvious result is that
" Chittagong, Kangra, and other districts " are getting
better prices for their teas. There is nothing in atmospheric action to generate or develop from the component
parts of the soil sufficient suitable food for plant-life,
and the production of tea-leaf, when once the necessary
elements are exhausted. The capability of the soil
for growing leaf was at its greatest when the first
planting began ; and all operations since have drawn
upon this supply, until there is in many cases but a very
little of it remaining. In the meanwhile, other gardens
starting in virgin land, with a full capital of fertility,
have brought their first fruits into the markets, and
coming from new soil of course have obtained higher
prices. It has been remarked to me as strange, that the
old concerns seem to suffer more than the new ones ;
but it would have been far stranger if they did not.
And when I have said—to people who had the best
possible reason for hoping it was not the case— that the
land, having been regularly worked out, was nearly used

up, they refused to admit this on any grounds, saying that the weather had been unfavourable, money scarce, or blight prevalent. A similar falling off was recently noticed by the London press in the tobacco lands of Havana. They have been drawn on so constantly, and given, if any, only a little manure, that now the lands are exhausted. Land in Sumatra, after giving one crop of tobacco is rested for four or five years. I am aware that tobacco is of more drastic growth than tea, but the same principle applies to both, in proportion. Whether the theory advanced by Dr. Schrottky as to the causes of red-spider blight was right or not, I cannot say; but he is borne out by scientific testimony in his verdict that the result of growing tea for years without manure is that the soil must become exhausted, and its produce almost valueless. In an early number of the *Indian Tea Gazette*, he wrote with perfect truth :

" The greater portion of the tea consumed in, and sent out of, India for the last fifteen or twenty years,— has it not been grown without a particle of manure ? has not the soil of the majority of tea-gardens year after year been deprived of its mineral plant-food, which, in the very best soil, seldom exceeds ten per cent. of the whole ? And can anyone be surprised now to find the plants getting every year weaker and weaker . . . . ? Do the shareholders in tea companies, happily deluded by the receipt of large dividends, know that these dividends represent a portion of the capital of the concern, and that they do not represent the real interest ? Do they know that shares, the real value of which is

Rs. 100 to-day, must next year be worth a definite amount less, paid away in dividends ?—for do they not sell, in every maund of tea, a portion of their garden ? (I speak, of course, only of companies which grow their tea either entirely without manuring, or manure only partially and inadequately.)"

If this is not the cause of the deterioration that un-questionably has been observed, it would be eminently satisfactory to know what is. A period of drought, or a visitation of blight, does not decrease the average price of tea per pound year by year, and affect old gardens more than young ones. Planters at the present time, are, at the very least, quite as capable as they were years ago ; so this falling off in quality cannot be attributed to lax supervision. Certainly, there have been seasons of commercial depression, in which money has seemed to be ruinously scarce : but I have trade testimony to the effect that, while admitting this, such teas as realised high prices in the market ten or fifteen years ago, do not now arrive from the then flourishing gardens.

It is contrary to all rational principles of maintenance to suppose that land can continue to be fertile for an indefinite number of years, in the total absence of any restorative agency whatever. Look where we will, we see in things necessary to our use the need of supplying decreased force, or, where doing so is out of our power, compulsory abandonment. Farm-lands, orchards, and even conservatories, require stimulants for their soils to maintain their vigour, just as men and animals need food to retain theirs. We have it on the authority of

Linnæus that minerals grow; and the exhaustion of mines is merely man's complete stoppage of the growth of nature by using up whatever Nature has stored. Diamonds will continue to grow where Nature has commenced the process, until man opens the earth and interferes with the development—then Nature will stop. What is sometimes advanced as being the self-generative principle in the fertility of soils is nowise in the same ratio as the exhaustion which goes on in tea-production. If complete impoverishment of tea soils did not eventually result from years of unrequited calls upon their fertility, Nature would reveal an exception to her own rules, and lower herself to the level of man's ingenuity.

This seems to me to be one cause of inferior tea. Although impoverished soil of course ranks first, another cause is to be found, in many instances, in inadequate pruning. I remember standing by a planter who was supervising his pruning on a Central Assam garden, and when remarking on the great size of the bushes, and the gnarled wood, he replied, " To prune some of these bushes *properly*, and as they *require* pruning, nearly an hour with saw and knife would be necessary, and, could it be given, the result would be magnificent." It was impossible not to agree with him. I had and have seen precisely the same thing in many instances, but I know how useless it is, in most cases, to hope to accomplish what is known to be necessary. When labour is limited, pruning is sometimes done by giving each cooly a number of bushes; and the result is to be imagined where gangs of people are at work in different directions, for the manager can only be in one place at a time.   More often than not, levelling the top of a bush and cutting out the twigs and wood made toward the close of the season, is all that can be done.   Extraordinary results have been obtained by ample draining and heavy pruning combined ; but planters cannot achieve victories without labour.

The very elaborate attention that is often given to tea-house details is frequently well-nigh useless, because earlier stages of work do not give a basis for perfect manufacturing arrangements to play on.   It is not of much use having scientific withering accommodation when the leaf to be withered has been grown on used-up soil, and lacks the essentials of good tea.   In my previous work I tried to show the importance of careful manufacture ; but the subject I am now writing on compels me to say that good leaf—which can only be obtained from well-nourished soil—is of primary importance in order that manufacture may give a satisfactory result.   Better results would often be obtained if more coolies were on the garden to effect improvements beyond hoeing, such as cutting drains, terracing, removing shade, &c.   And this brings me to a point which has to be noticed— namely, a way in which many people might be released from the tea-house and put on outdoor work.   I refer to the labour requirements for sieving.   If this phase of tea-house work were abolished, many gardens would benefit immensely.   Planters follow each other in the practice of sorting their teas into classes because it is the regular custom, everyone doing it.   But while I should be extremely sorry to seek to upset any useful process in vogue in tea-houses at the present time, I think I may perhaps notice that of sieving, with possibly a good result. Just for a moment, for the reason explained at foot, I will refer to the present mode of working and the sieves in use. I believe it is customary to use No. 10 or 12 mesh for Pekoe. (I have known No. 8 to be used, but only in two factories.) Now a Pekoe leaf (manufactured tea) is of greater length than can possibly pass through a space in the sieve used, when lying lengthways. To get through the aperture at all the leaf must be inverted; in being inverted, more probably than not the leaf is grated, the bloom lessened, and the leaf snapped or broken at the end. This is surely very undesirable, and the facts apply to Souchong at least equally with Pekoe. The sieves generally in use on tea factories would answer very well for some grains; but they are certainly not of the kind to allow long or wiry leaves to fall through gently by their own weight and size; to pass through at all they must first get on end.*

I fear I shall be surprising many planters in expressing my belief that it is an open question whether the

---

* This idea is not my own, but came up in the course of a conversation, on sifting, with Mr. Haworth, the rolling-machine inventor. I believe an improved sieve has been recently made for tea-house use, but I have been unable to obtain particulars of it at the time of going to press. Should any planters desire information on the subject, I am sure it will be readily furnished by Mr. W. Haworth, 7, Lothbury, London, E.C.

sorting of teas is not a waste of labour and money.
The expense is considerable in itself, especially when bad
weather for withering, or inferior flushes at the close of
the season, cause the leaf to break in rolling. If the
cost of sieving were done away with, the item of itself
would be a considerable saving ; but in releasing hands
for profitable outdoor work it would proportionately be
even a greater one. I know that some gardens send
their crops home unsifted, and from the continuance
of the practice it may be supposed to answer. It is
common enough during the rains in Assam and Cachar
to see sections of gardens in jungle, flushes harden-
ing on the bushes, and dozens of people occupied in
sifting tea. What a different state of affairs might
be were sifting done away with, or even partly so. More
people would be on the garden, tea would not have to
remain over in several varieties for more of each kind to
be sorted before breaks could be packed. After manufacture it could be given a brisk final firing (if necessary)
and packed off, to its more effectual retention of strength
and aroma, I am sure. Quality would run pretty evenly,
too, because tea made during a spell of fine or unfavourable weather would be packed at once and all
together. A few more boxes would perhaps be required,
as unsorted tea occupies more space than that which
has been crushed through sieves ; but the reduced cost
of wear and tear in this latter article would counter-
balance the expense of the former. What is the practical utility of sorting teas ? Class names do not
determine the price ; it is common enough in the sale-

rooms to see Pekoe of one estate sell for less than Souchong from another. There can be no doubt that Indian teas are principally used for mixing with Chinese teas. Seeing, then, that the retailer makes his own blends, and that the labour expended in Indian tea-houses virtually goes for nothing (Pekoe, Souchong, broken teas, dust, &c., being mixed up with one or more kinds of China teas), it seems to me to be of very questionable utility to send home teas sorted into classes, when before they get into the consumer's tea-pot their class-identity is destroyed. I have represented this matter to grocers in different parts of England, and the general reply has been that much trouble would be spared them, as they have to taste many teas, and open several chests, to make up their blends. Tea gets disfigured and broken about a great deal in factory sorting, warehouse bulking, and final blending by the retailer, and makes a quantity of small tea, or dust, which is not remunerative to the dealer. I think also that, if Indian tea stands any chance at all of being drunk alone from original packages, it will certainly be in this form : for while Pekoe would be too rough, Souchong might be too smooth, Broken Pekoe too rasping, and so on. But I have to refer to this point further on.

The fact of having noticed this matter renders it unnecessary for me to say that I believe it might be followed up, at all events to some extent, particularly as regards the months when Assam and Cachar planters are having their heaviest gatherings, and also making their finest teas ; because the good growing weather that brings out the leaves, brings up the jungle between the bushes, and the greatest pressure is often experienced for out-door labour. I would say, in passing from this point, that I am not endeavouring to revolutionise present tea-house arrangements, because most sudden changes are detrimental ; but I do think that unsorted teas might be sent home to a much greater extent than they are, and with very satisfactory results. Or, looking at the matter in a most indifferent light, the plan is worth trying. Farther on in this chapter I hope to show why it is imperatively necessary to produce tea at a less cost; and I think that to pack tea for a smaller outlay, and by so doing to obtain better results in the garden, would be true economy. The primary need for a successful result is good leaf—without which, manufacturing arrangements are of quite a secondary value ; and while not forgetting my previous remarks as to impoverished soil, planters will bear me out when I say that the best soil loses its value when denied good cultivation. I think that in many cases the suggestion will be applicable to give more attention than is frequently now given to the production of the leaf, even it were at the expense of manufacture. The demand that existed ten years ago for pretty teas and silvery tips has become modified almost to extinction. *Useful* teas are the valuable ones now ; and good, solid strength, or fine flavour, with a modicum of external roughness and unfinish, will be far more marketable than an elegant tea lacking these essentials. Consumers rarely look into the caddy at the appearance of their tea ; they do not like it to be so small as to pass into the cup, but otherwise strength and flavour in the infusion constitute the merits.

I will now endeavour to notice the feasibility of carrying into practice the general demand from Indian planters for their tea to be drunk by itself. The first point that seems to require notice is that planters, from any district whatever, invariably believe that, for some reason or other, their tea is superior to all others, that it is a great injustice to mix it with China tea, and is almost second-hand nectar for drinking alone. Having myself been a vigorous partisan of this way of thinking, I can hardly be considered a novice in the matter ; and I feel quite sorry to have to shatter the Penates of the planter's mental home, by saying that the demand is unreasonable. Planters whose only experience of Indian tea has been obtained in Assam, or districts where the strongest kinds are grown, have no idea of the really fine, delicate-flavoured teas that are sent to England from other districts — teas that undoubtedly are well-suited for drinking alone—which those from Assam, Cachar, and Sylhet, as a rule, are not. Many planters in the former place have broken Souchong, or even fannings, for their own use. How would they like to drink the Pekoe they make in favourable weather in June and July ? I know of a case where one of the London staff of an Indian tea company brought himself into a mental condition similar to *delirium tremens* through alcohol, by drinking Indian

8 *

Pekoe tea too freely.   The gentleman was an abstainer from intoxicants, and naturally felt hurt when his doctor said he had incipient *delirium tremens*.   Such, however, was the case; and although the term was not applicable in Dr. Blake's rendering of the expression—"the brain fever of drunkards"—it was certainly the preliminary stage of what Dr. Elliotson has called "*delirium cum tremore*."   No Assam planter could reasonably expect people to drink his Pekoe.   With a few exceptions, Indian teas are far too pungent to be drunk alone. Congou, as made plentifully some years ago, was about the nicest drinking Assam tea.   I well know the regular cries about Indian teas being far more economical than Chinese ones, and I believe in, and advocate, the practice wherever I can—but only as applied to Neilgherry, Kangra Valley, or finer Darjeeling teas. Some of the produce from these districts is delicious, and possesses a delicacy of flavour which cannot be compared with anything coming from Assam.   I dare say this will be exceedingly unpalatable to planters in the old province; and I am told by a few retired growers who know that I am writing thus, that the sentiment will not be appreciated; but having myself at one time loudly cried out against the (almost) iniquity of mixing Assam tea with "nasty rubbish" from China, and seeing now how impracticable it is to expect anything else— seeing, also, that it is in this very respect that Assam teas are valuable—I think it would be a mistaken kindness not to tell the truth on the matter.   And I think, too, that it must be added, that all the laments on the subject

have availed but little.   Pungent Indian teas have been
wanted, as they generally are, have been bought as
usual, and applied to the purpose for which they were
bought ; but the growers have, in many cases, thought
themselves ill-treated.   It will not be soothing to them
to be now told that Kangra and other " comparatively insignificant districts " grow tea that is put to the
use that Assam growers think *their* teas are specially
qualified for.   But what is the converse ?   Kangra
Valley teas, whilst (with the exception of some of its
Pekoes) very drinkable by themselves, are of but little
use in the purposes that render Assam and Cachar
teas absolutely incomparable.   A good market has long
existed, and continues to exist, for the strong growths
of India to fortify weaker China and Java teas, and
for this purpose, year after year, the tea that reaches
London is sold.   Supposing planters restricted the sale
for this purpose—as many would, if they could afford
it—what would be the result ?   Where would people be
found to drink the teas that planters themselves do not
drink because of their strength ?   There is no doubt as
to the injurious effects of over-strong tea—who would
drink those from India ?   Such teas when infused cannot
be diluted into a pleasant drink ; for when they are
watered copiously the result is a thin, rasping, bitter
liquor, in no way mellow or nice.   Can planters expect
people to go out of their way to such an extent as this ?
Surely not.   The growers of these strong, rasping,
pungent teas, virtually hold a monopoly against the
whole world.   Such teas are produced nowhere out of

India.   Tea to be drunk unmixed must necessarily be
of but medium strength.   China, Japan, and Java
export weak tea in hundreds of millions of pounds
annually; do Indian planters, possessing at this moment
advantages obtainable nowhere else, wish their produce
to descend to the level of the teas they so vigorously
decry ?   Instead of despising China tea because it is
weak, and thin, and impure, they ought to be thankful
that it is so bad, because therein exists the safety of
their present unassailable position.   Tea that is weak
enough, and poor enough, and common enough, to be
drunk alone without injury from its excessive strength, is
the outcome of cultivation and manufacture in China of
a kind in which Indian planters have no belief whatever.
Remembering that it is absolutely impossible for people
to drink for any length of time tea that is of extra
strength and pungency, do the planters of Assam and
Cachar desire that their teas should become common-
place, ranking with those from China, and that they
should pass out from the unassailable position they
occupy as the growers of tea that cannot be elsewhere
produced ?   Either this, or the stereotyped cry results
from insufficient consideration.   Which is the better :—
to grow tea that cannot be produced in any other part of
the world, and have it used for fortifying China tea which
year by year becomes more in need of fortifying, and
to send it to a market where it is always saleable for this
purpose—a purpose which no other teas can supply—
or to have the forty or fifty millions of pounds which
reach home this season, take rank with teas that are

sometimes so common as to be chiefly valuable because of the duty paid upon them?

Briefly, then, it seems to me that this matter stands thus:—Many Indian planters, while finding their teas too strong for their own drinking, have through insufficiently reasoning the matter out, thought that Indian tea might be drunk alone, and that an injustice was done to the industry in using their teas for fortifying weaker China ones. But as some of the Indian growths are much too strong for use by themselves, and as a large proportion of the China tea imports into England require strengthening, these strong growths from India—which cannot be used alone—are valuable for giving strength to inferior China teas, and for this reason only. Indian teas of unpalatable strength preponderate over those of medium strength. If they are not to be used for mixing with China teas, what is to be done with them? But for so mixing them, there would be no market for them; and planting in the Kangra Valley, and other districts named, would stand an exclusive chance of success, should mixing Indian with China tea be discontinued.

One reason against the use of Indian tea by itself, and I consider it the principal one, arises from the great natural strength of the leaf. The next reason I almost think I may call a fungus on the tree of domestic economy, in that it is not a natural, a reasonable, or a profitable growth. Very generally throughout the United Kingdom, and particularly in the suburbs of London, for some time past, there has been a

low-priced tea mania. Competition in trade has become
so keen—suicidal almost—that in the sale of tea, Dis-
raeli's satire on competition (in "Popanilla," I think) is
almost verified, as people receive presents for buying
the tea at all. There has developed a great variety of
such inducements. Magazine Tea Companies, Book
Bonus Tea Companies, and others giving glass and tin
ware, pictures, ornaments, and sundry articles, with each
packet of tea purchased. These shops generally sell tea
only—and, as is well known, in an ordinary way retailed
tea carries a good profit. It is strange to think that
people patronise such patent deceptions—or, being-patent,
I suppose they cannot be called deceptions—but there can
be no doubt that these article-giving companies do an
enormous business, and take from legitimate traders one
of their principal supports—the sale of tea. I remember
reading in (I think) the *Grocer*, some time since, that in
the north of England some tradesmen were "giving
away" two pounds of sugar to each purchaser of a
pound of tea. The result of all this in London and
many of the large towns is that grocers have been compelled to offer their teas at the very lowest prices possible,
and their returns being thus lessened, they have not been
able to pay the price for tea that they formerly could.
The consumer has been the gainer in all this, and the
grower the greatest loser ; the retailer probably has
bought for less money, but his profits on his outlay have
been smaller. But the strangest part of the whole
affair seems to be that not only in the neighbourhoods
of artisans and working people, but in those representing

a higher social status, persons have now become accustomed to expect a really good tea for very little money. It is an odd phase of public expectation; very disadvantageous to the grower, and unsatisfactory for the grocer. The editor of a London weekly journal, who had lived for some years in Russia, in speaking to me recently of the difficulty of obtaining good tea in England, said that this general belief in cheap tea constituted one of the strange notions that occupy the public mind from time to time. Persons whose consumption of tea is very small, strongly object to paying a few pence per pound beyond a low price to obtain much better tea, when the addition at the most would be but the cost of a cab-fare for a short distance, which they would not think twice about incurring. Also, where gentlemen would never think of telling their guests that the wine was cheap, and would feel hurt if anyone suggested that this was the case, rather feeling proud to know it was costly, ladies, ruling the other side of the domestic structure, pride themselves upon what they like to believe is good tea at a low figure, and persistently refuse to advance the price. "Like to believe," I say. I must not cast doubt on the tea, as it is not long since I saw labelled in a west-end shop, " Good Indian tea 1s. 4d. per lb." It was not an exhilarating sight. I purchased some of the tea, and remembering the hands it had passed through profitably, from the broker downward, was loath to confess that it was very good value for the money to the consumer, but ruinously little money for the value to the grower. With a large section of the public determined not to advance its price, Indian tea (which realises a higher all-round average than China tea) cannot be offered for sale as a regular thing, and in the entirety of its exportation, at anything like the price the public is now only prepared to give. This 1s. 4d. tea, I think I may say, was exceptional—at least I hope so—but the general public, in the masses, would not give the prices now realised for the finer Indian teas, for the low-price mixtures seem to have obtained the mastery of the public reason, and inflated the general housekeeper with principles cheap and nasty. Grocers have told me that they would be virtually closing their doors for the sale of tea if they were only to offer high-priced Indian produce. The day has passed when tea was the beverage of the wealthy only; but the masses refuse to understand that a tea at 2s. 6d. per lb., which goes nearly double as far as a weak one at 1s. 8d. or 1s. 10d. per lb., is really the cheaper. A Bonus Tea Company will, perhaps, give a tin tea-pot to the purchaser of a pound of 2s. tea; the *bonâ fide* grocer cannot give a tea-pot, so he gives a better tea at 2s., or the same as the Bonus Company's at 1s. 10d. People see Bonus Companies and grocers running low prices, and forthwith believe that it is a mistake to pay a high price for tea. To meet this belief, as I have said, the grocer is compelled to pay less (which, of course, lessens the sale price and affects the grower); and to make the best blends he can at the prices limited by his customers, he puts in as much strong Indian tea as can be afforded, with a balance of weak leafy China tea. Therefore, even if all Indian teas were sufficiently palatable to be drunk alone, grocers at the present time could not obtain from the masses of the people such prices as are realised in the sale-rooms. It is manifestly, then, to the grower's interest to let the grocer have the tea for his own purpose, or otherwise there will be no demand for the strongest Indian teas.

There have been various efforts made in London to establish retail depôts for the sale of Indian teas, and for the direct consignment of crops, in order to do away with all middlemen, and to make the grower the retailer. The usual reasons given for inaugurating such establishments have been, that old Indians prefer Indian to China tea, that in the past they have experienced great difficulty in obtaining really good tea save at exorbitant prices, that Indian tea is infinitely superior to China tea—a fact beyond question—and that the intelligent public have long been unfairly treated in that pure Indian teas have been withheld from them, &c., and various similar assertions which pretty fairly covered up the fact that old Indians were really not catered for any more than other sections of the public, and that the principal reason for opening these establishments was to make money, by keeping the Broker and wholesale dealer out of the field. As a most natural sequence, most of these efforts have failed. They have taken form in shops, packet companies, &c., but have not succeeded. Certainly a few remain, but their continued existence is very exceptional and is to be accounted for specially. It cannot reasonably be expected that a few retail tea-shops scattered about London, could educate the public taste to prefer tea that growers themselves do not care to drink. Very little tea, indeed, from India requires strength to be added; so where the palatable teas might be sold for unmixed use, there would be an immense surplus of strong teas. The consumption of, say fifty millions of pounds, cannot be aided to any extent worth thinking of by a few retail shops. If a giant company organised a system of having an Indian tea-shop in every town in the United Kingdom, but a fraction of the Indian crop would be disposed of. Let anyone notice the number of grocers in any mile of main thoroughfare in London; and remembering that probably each is selling Indian tea in his blends, and so maintaining the demand for it, try to reckon how much (or little) use a shop here and there would be. I admit that Indian tea-shops might be made to pay for themselves, but their aid to the industry would be represented by a decimal fraction. Many efforts have been made to push the sale of Indian tea by irregular channels, but with very little permanent success. A few years ago grocers were sometimes willing to take small crops for sale on commission ; but they can buy now more advantageously in the regular way. Brokers and public auction represent the only adequate means of disposal of the Indian crop, looked at as a whole. A man having a small estate might retail his crop in England, but his returns would be slow in coming ; and viewing the industry above individual cases, the produce must go through the regular trade channels for efficient distribution, and such channels are undoubtedly the best. The requirements of the United Kingdom are represented in the Mincing Lane sale-rooms. What are a few isolated shops against such a centralised organisation? Beside which, how simple is the plan now in vogue of making tea over to Brokers for sale and receiving the proceeds; what an easy system of realisation this is as compared with the tedious details of a retail community, with a certain proportion of bad debts.

I must just for a moment again refer to old Indians. Old Indians like being catered for beyond a doubt; it generally pleases any man to be considered a connoisseur. In point of fact, old Indians or anyone else need not have the smallest difficulty in obtaining Indian teas, as nearly all the London Co-operative stores keep a good stock, some of them even going in for district growths. Old Indians like to get inside an Indian tea-shop and *gup*—there can be no doubt about that—but it often happens that old Indians possess (or are possessed by) *Mem-sahibs*, who like to arrange for their own tea. They, too, have lived in India, and know what tea is. This regard for the comfort of elderly " Qui Hais " has caught a good many of them, I know; but I have heard it remarked upon as strange that there are not corresponding " damper " shops for ex-Australians, " sangaree " taps for returning West Indians, with an occasional " Baked young woman " dining-room for travelling African gentlemen. From what I have seen of old Indians, I cannot help thinking that if they particularly wanted Indian tea and could not get it in London, India not being a very long way off, they would soon have

what they wished.   But then it is very pleasant to be
catered for.

A questionably judicious variety exists in the packages
containing tea sent home.   That the same thing is
done in China is not necessarily a recommendation,
I think.   Small boxes, excepting about the time of
Christmas sales, are generally of no standard value.
A twenty-pound caddy of Assam Pekoe might be a
rather costly present ; but it would be likely to make the
recipients think that the Assam soil possessed some
remarkable properties, or else that the black people
were not altogether aromatic ; for I think no one would
very long care to drink such tea as a regular thing.
There is but little demand for these small cases of tea
if they have to be put up to public auction ; they may or
may not sell well, but larger cases are preferable.   I do
not mean of the ungainly size sent home some years
ago from one district, and which obtained the eupho-
nious appellation in the market of " Kangra Coffins."
No small quantity of tea is coming home just now in
one-pound lead-foil packets.   Some of the London shops
are selling these teas (Darjeeling and Cachar are all I
have seen), and I am told the packets sell fairly well as
novelties ; but the practice must necessarily be restricted,
seeing that Indian teas are required in bulk for mixing.
The masses of the people do not buy tea by the pound,
and as the public taste varies greatly in different parts
of England, grocers must be allowed to blend for themselves to meet this taste.   A soft delicate flavoured tea
is not suited for places where the water is hard, or a

rasping one where it is the reverse. These matters cannot be worked from India.

The idea prevails somewhat generally in the tea districts that Indian teas are not sufficiently well known, that things for planters might be much brighter if grocers and the public were more generally aware of the superiority of Indian tea. All I can say regarding the trade is that the tea could not have been sold in Mincing Lane for forty years, and in millions of pounds annually, without being pretty well known; and although but a small proportion of the public ask their grocers for Indian teas, it is used in the shop mixtures The majority of grocers now advertise "Indian and China Tea," or "Assam and China Tea," and people can get Indian tea readily enough by asking for it, if they are willing to pay the grocer's price. Beyond this, retailers do not push Indian tea, because experience has shown that generally the public either dislike the price or grumble at the flavour—really meaning the strength. Of course a more marked demand for such teas as are suitable for drinking alone would greatly help the industry; and if every planter in India would prevail upon his friends at home to drink Indian tea only, some good might be effected. But then Indian planters are egotistical, and probably each would tell his friends to be sure to get *his* district tea. This is, of course, perfectly natural; it would be odd indeed if we did not believe in the superiority of our own work. I know a tea establishment which bought a chest of Dehra Doon tea for an old Indian who walked in one day and asked for some, vouchsafing at the same time the information that there was no Indian tea so good. He had the chest to himself, in small quantities from time to time, as no one else inquired for Dehra Doon tea. A similar case occurred in the same place, when two old gentlemen entered and asked to see some "Kakkar" tea. As the assistant could not quite see what they really wanted, he showed them the first Indian tea that was to hand. One of the inquirers took a leaf, nibbled it, and exclaimed triumphantly to his friend, "Ah! yes, this is it—I recognise the flavour; you can't beat the Kakkar tea all over India." An order was given, and Cachar tea sent. Belief in the virtues of district teas is very strong.

A somewhat similar fear to that last noticed is occasionally expressed that young estates do not stand an ordinarily good chance of patronage. This is a mistake. The London market is extremely fair, and provided sufficiently large breaks are sent, planters may rely upon their teas being tried, whatever the mark. The monopoly of old marks has passed away, and good tea will be found out, let its mark be what it may. At the same time I would just mention that it is an unpleasant thing for a mark to get a bad name, because it makes the sale of its teas very laboured. I just recal, in writing, a case in which four wholesale houses gave me the same characteristic as to the teas of one concern regarding which I had inquired. Now I knew that teas from several estates were packed under one mark, with a distinguishing capital letter, and it was impossible for all the factories regularly to commit the same error in manufacture ; yet, unfortunately, that was the trade belief. Not that the teas were always so—they were acknowledged to be of good strength—but they were very likely to be affected, as mentioned to me. Indian teas as a class stand in high appreciation in the market. I was in the sale-rooms one morning just as the first new China teas were arriving, and a brisk-looking individual, with his hat on the back of his head and a catalogue in his hand, remarked, " It is quite a treat to come to the Indians after the Monings ; " and from the worthy man's bidding I concluded that he was very glad. On this occasion some of the Kangra Valley Pekoes fetched higher prices than Assam ones of old marks. I thought of the heavily-taxed soil.

Before passing from this subject of sales and disposal, I am anxious to notice briefly the relative positions of Planters and Brokers. I do not know what the latter generally think of the former, but I do know what the former think of the latter in very many cases—that they know very little about tea, and are unable to have any particularly keen interest in teas made over to them, because of the short time they are in hand. Both ideas are altogether wrong. Brokers are but too glad for the teas they sell to realise well, and they have the interest of the industry at heart certainly as much as the majority of planters. It is oftentimes by no means an easy matter for brokers to dispose of teas ; and there is a large amount of quiet pushing, and endeavouring to secure the highest figure possible, particularly when teas are withdrawn from sales and have afterward to be disposed

9

of privately. Planters' and brokers' interests are manifestly identical—one cannot do without the other—and
the wish of each for the advancement of the industry
arises from the same cause, and its success is mutually
beneficial. There is not less proportionate labour to the
broker to sell teas for a low price, than there is to the
planter to produce it for so selling; and a dull market
is as serious for the one as for the other. As for brokers
not understanding tea, it seems a very absurd thing
to notice, but the expression is by no means rare in
India. Brokers are not tea-planters, I admit; but it
is in no way necessary for them to be. If good tea is
sent home, the trade will recognise and buy it; but it is
unreasonable to charge brokers with not understanding
tea because they cannot readily sell such as are sour,
burnt, or flat. The fact that year by year the disposal
of the Indian crop is effected, is surely sufficient testimony
to the efficiency of London brokers. It is often said in
India that, as brokers do not understand cultivation and
manufacture, they cannot know much about tea. This
is ridiculous. It is not necessary for a bootmaker to be
a grazier to be able to tell whether a piece of manufactured leather will wear well. If tea is bad, it ought
to be sufficient for the broker to look to the planter about
it, and just say what is wrong. Before passing to my
next section of management, I should like to explain my
meaning in this matter more clearly, if I can, by a very
homely simile. When a tea-planter has been drinking
bottled beer daily for some years, he thinks himself able
to say when beer is good or bad, and it does not seem

necessary to him to be a brewer to decide that question. And should a case of beer be bad, he thinks it quite sufficient to tell the consignor of the fact. Further, he feels himself qualified to express an opinion on the subject, notwithstanding that he is not a practical brewer. The same rule surely holds good with brokers and tea.

What I have to say on the subject of management as connected with production, will seem, I fear, at first a little one-sided, although actually it aims as much at the benefit of owners and agents as at the planter's. I think that oftentimes managers are considered responsible for what it is quite out of their power to control, and are expected to bring about results to which nature is altogether opposed. It is not unfrequently believed that because a man makes good tea on one garden, he must succeed in the same thing on another; or the manager of an estate may have his life made miserable by being constantly written to regarding the good prices obtained by a neighbouring planter, and by queries as to why he cannot also obtain a similar result. While I would not for a moment endeavour to lessen the credit a planter may secure for making good tea, I would say that all managers are primarily dependent for success upon the natural conditions of their gardens. Good tea cannot be made from leaf grown in poor or unsuitable soil; and there is sometimes to be seen the greatest diifference in the producing capabilities of two gardens situated side by side. Where one, being favoured by nature, obtains

9 *

good prices, the other, with nature against it, or less favourable to it, ought not, because of its inevitable result, bring blame to the manager. Owners—and often enough even planters, too, for that matter—seem to suppose that their particular tea ought to obtain at least as high a price as any in the market. This is most unreasonable. A planter who obtains good prices for tea made on, say, an eight-year old Assam garden, should not be expected to be able to make equally good tea from an unmanured and proportionably exhausted Cachar garden a quarter of a century old. The mania of earlier years caused tea to be planted in places which would not be looked at now; but where such gardens remain, it is useless to expect from them a return of a hundred-fold. A careless system of manufacture, a low standard of cultivation, and ignorant neglect, may certainly be avoided; but it is very unreasonable to expect a planter to make good tea, and blame him for failure, when nature, or the class of plant in the garden, excludes the possibility of success. It is possible to assist nature, in draining, trenching, &c., but a manager with a garden of low *ját* plant in stiff clayey soil, stands no chance against a garden of good plant in friable soil. I have never met a planter who was not too glad to make the very best tea he could consistently with his estimated out-turn. It is unpleasant enough to have one's neighbours getting the highest prices, but to be blamed for this when everything else is impossible, is particularly hard. Other cases of extreme unfairness to planters occur, which might oftentimes be

averted and prevented, if agents and owners had a more
accurate knowledge of tea-planting, or, not having this,
would allow themselves to be guided by their managers.
A planter may sometimes see that the garden needs a
heavy pruning to ensure its later out-turn, and he acts
on his conviction. A reduced crop in the following
season results, agents become dissatisfied, and " reluc-
tantly " dispense with the manager. All they want is
success—*i.e* an increasing crop: shareholders are not
satisfied with a report of heavy pruning, blight, or bad
weather, in lieu of dividend ; so the manager who, acting
conscientiously and consistently for the garden's future
benefit, made a short out-turn as a stepping-stone thereto,
is dispensed with, and a new man installed. The result,
of course, is a good crop of fine leaf from new wood, which
makes (or ought to make) capital tea : the new manager
is credited with his success, and the agents are confirmed
in their estimate of the previous one as inefficient :
which estimate, more probably than not, goes the round
of tea people in Calcutta. *Vivat Justitia !*

Considerable unpleasantness often occurs through
factory estimates. Planters estimate for quantity under
orders, and (to my own knowledge) have been told to
estimate 60 per cent. of Pekoe. Now any planter could
make this percentage easily enough if he were able to
pluck at his own discretion ; but his practical knowledge goes for nothing against that of persons who
could not distinguish the *Thea Assamica* from the *Coffea
Arabica*. The only course left to a planter so placed, is
to pluck heavily without regard to the next season,

obtain what Pekoe he can by legitimate sifting, and make up the 60 per cent. by crushing good marketable Souchong through the Pekoe sieve. In estimating expenditure, the probable cost of every item of factory expense is oftentimes expected to be calculated to a fraction, and allowances for incidental expenses, which are absolutely certain to occur, are generally cut out. This kind of thing is frequently carried out at the expense of efficiency, or if broken through, only to cause unpleasantness. In out-turn, also, estimating is often overdone ; a good one is wanted to put in the annual report, often to cover the shortcomings of the previous year's actual. Hail-storms, blight, cholera, loss of garden-labour by fires, or bad weather, cannot be estimated for—but they ought to be allowed for, as one or the other is almost certain to occur. The *emyloyés* of large concerns occasionally have the misfortune to lose a reputation it has taken years of hard work to build up, by being transferred to a district they know nothing of. They find a difference in language, climate, seasons, and mode of manufacture, and from unavoidable ignorance obtain a result far less satisfactory than had been expected.

It has been said with, I think, not a little truth, that much of the success of the prosperous tea companies is due to the retention of one staff. For many reasons this is greatly to be desired, as planters become thoroughly acquainted with the natural condition of the soil, the capacity of the bushes, are known by the coolies, and this familiarity produces good results.

Gardens in a critical condition are often in no way improved by a sudden change of management. President Lincoln used to say that it was a mistake to change horses when crossing a stream; and the principle stands good in many cases of the re-organization of failing tea estates. Much expense, injustice, and disappointment might be saved, if, before believing a man incompetent, owners would obtain professional testimony as to whether a garden were capable of doing any better than it had done. Because an estate does not make progress, it in no way follows that the manager is inefficient This will be a rather difficult point to agree upon, I da say; but it is only a just view. No planter, however skilful, can work wonders with a garden that suffers—as many gardens do—from insurmountable natural disadvantages; neither can any planter, of any reputation or capacity whatsoever, do justice to himself if kept short of labour.

I would just notice the feeling of mutual trust and union that unfortunately is sometimes wanting between the working executive of an estate. Often enough owners grumble, and say other peoples' estates give far better results, and what their agents are doing they don't know. Agents are aggrieved, and say, that do what they will, they can never work cheaply enough for some people. Planters are worried by the voracity of the owner-agent element, and believe that if their bushes flushed every other day all the year round, they would be accomplishing too little if they did not bring about a special flush on Sunday! And so the executive goes on—a Mutual Grievance Society. This common state of affairs is very much to be regretted, the more so as it often results from ignorance. Owners are frequently not financial agents, agents are not planters, and planters are not keeping up London houses on the proceeds of the estates they manage. Neither party understands the way in which the other reasons or calculates, and dissatisfaction results. If owners would be more reasonable than they very often are, and would worry agents less than they very often do, agents in their turn would have fewer extraordinary requests to make to planters, and planters fewer unleavened observations to make to their neighbours, as to owners and agents both. Seeing that neither section is really independent of the other, how very much better it would be if, by the introduction of a little mutual trust, the working were carried on harmoniously. The owner may rely on his estate solely for his income ; but, while the planter's relation to the garden is precisely the same, and the agent's partly so, surely the very best reasons exist for each section to leave the other alone, to a proper extent, trusting to the powerful law of financial self-preservation to accomplish all that is needful. I say to a proper extent, because, of course, primarily the agents are the servants of the owners, and the planter of both, although directly responsible to the former.

The very considerable decrease in the prices now obtained for Indian teas, compared with those which ruled even ten years ago, whilst resulting in many cases from inferior quality, may be also partly explained on the general ground that Indian tea has now fairly taken its place as a staple commodity, and can no longer command a somewhat fancy price as a *spécialité*. Although now and again small parcels of Pekoe still fetch remarkably high prices, the bulk of the Indian imports realise a price much nearer to that obtained for China tea than was formerly the case. As to the lower all-round averages there can be no doubt. Public faith in cheap tea seems, unfortunately, to be established ; and the prices of Indian growths, in addition to the unpalatable strength, render the sale of unmixed Indian tea extremely doubtful. It is in no way likely that market prices will materially advance from those ruling now— of course there will be the usual fluctuations in the sale-rooms—but the marketable value of Indian tea has now been fairly well ascertained, and one most important fact reveals itself therefrom, that as prices cannot go up, the cost of production must come down. Either this, or innumerable estates will become bankrupt. This cannot be considered a pessimist view, but a hard fact, which is supported by another—that, as I write, more than a few concerns have taken a new lease of hope because of an improvement in the tea-market. Produc tion, then, must be cheaper—how is it to be done ? I am perfectly well assured that every tea estate in India has been worked at the closest allowance possible for some time : so that to introduce economy beyond this, will seem almost an impossibility. But I think it will be possible to work more economically in one or two directions, although, perhaps, the monthly outlay of money will not be less. I would say first, considering the probable bankruptcy of the soil of many gardens—of which steadily falling prices, against higher ones for new estate teas, are sufficient corroboration—let an agricultural analytical chemist be employed to ascertain what properties of the soils of different gardens have been most drawn on, and manures be scientifically constructed to replenish the impoverished land. I write thus after careful personal inquiry on the subject, and would caution owners and agents against the use of general manures, such as are recommended for other crops. The essential component parts of good tea should be ascertained on a scale, and worked upon as a standard; soil should be analysed, and a manure made to add to it, in proper proportions, such needful elements as are lacking. It has been urged upon me by agriculturists that this would be an expensive procedure, especially in large estates; but as it seems to me to be virtually countenancing the bankruptcy of the soil to withhold active measures for its replenishment, I do not think such an important and needful expenditure should be kept back. And the working of this system would be really very easy. The properties wanting in the soil to provide the elements of good tea would not be numerous, and the manures necessary for different gardens could be made by rule-of-three calculations. The exhausted properties would vary in different gardens, but as the basis of manure would be the same for all—to produce tea— it would be easy enough to add more of one element and less of another, so as to put in each garden such drugs as ought to be consumed by the bushes in the production of superior leaf. A properly qualified analyst could make a tour of the different districts, and examine the soils of tea estates ; the analysis would show what properties were wanting, and also their proportion, and a manure could be made up in Calcutta—it would probably be blending the same materials in different proportions for different gardens —and, as made, it could be packed, marked, and shipped. In this way, soils could be brought up to the possession of full capacity for producing tea-leaf of requisite strength. Beyond the cost of manure, there would be no expense for obtaining from areas now under cultivation a largely-increased out-turn ; therefore I say that although the monthly expenses would not be less, the result would really be economical.

This is one way of cheapening production- -by obtaining a greater result from an existing area at a proportionately smaller cost. Another way, it seems to me, is the abandoment of many sections of gardens that are altogether unremunerative, unless it should be decided to manure them amply. I can call to mind at this moment large sections of several gardens, with a greater percentage of vacancies than of plants, and which were regularly hoed in the round, and hoed at a loss, for the leaf obtained was scarcely worth the cost of plucking it. Such sections, worked at a loss, or even if not cultivated at a profit, would pay better in being closed, or kept only for seed, with an occasional hoeing I remember sections of this kind that had been regularly hoed for years,

and the plants have been so scarce, that when eventually
" filling up vacancies " had been taken in hand, no
trace of the original lines could be found, and re-plant-
ing had to be done to fill up vacancies. This latter
work, too, is one that is oftentimes carried on upon
unsound principles of agriculture. Where bushes have
slowly died out from want of adequate plant-food, seeds
or seedlings are planted. This work of filling up vacancies has misled many people, because the seedlings have
got on so satisfactorily, causing hopes to be entertained
of an eventually flourishing garden. Does not this
progress of seedlings contradict what I say? Not at
all. The case is simply that a child can develop upon
an amount of food which would not save a man's life;
and plants that are growing for three years without
being plucked, are like people who, being fed without
giving work in return, need less food than a more active
member. I know cases can be shown where vacancy
filling has been a complete success; but more often
than not, such vacancies have arisen through the bushes
being killed by bad hoeing, or by the borer, or through
neglected cultivation, and not through impoverished soil.
But at the best the work is risky; and I think it would
be a wise plan before beginning it, to submit a sample
of the soil to an agricultural analyst, for examination as
to whether it is capable of nourishing bushes fit to
be plucked, and not merely of developing seedling life.
Many gardens would derive great advantage if the labour
at present wasted on exhausted land were bestowed
on them; higher cultivation would give more leaf

and better leaf; and a larger return from a smaller area, I submit, would be greater economy than obtaining a smaller out turn from a larger area. Then there are out-gardens of many concerns which have never paid— estates varying from forty to, perhaps, eighty acres, worked at a loss year after year. This is not the time for drawing on the Hope Branch of the Collapse Company. If these numerous out-gardens have not paid in past times, unless there is a large amount of young tea coming into bearing, it may pretty safely be said that they never will pay. And if a garden does not pay, or in young tea has not a near chance of paying, working it is useless. Such outlyings might be sold or leased. There are planters who would rather work on a lease-held garden with a chance of making a profit on their own working, than draw a salary year after year without a chance of making more money. Or, if Europeans could not be found, natives would be ready to work in this way; and even five hundred rupees annually in rental would be far better than the empty dignity of possession in a garden worked at a loss. In advocating economy, I know I am harping upon an old string; but I hope I advocate real, possible economy, and not the gnat-straining parsimony of cutting a Rs. 6 per month Chowkeydar from the Bungalow establishment, or refusing Rs. 50 per mensem to a hard-working planter, while acres of land are year after year worked at a dead loss. Some concerns have gone on for years extending and cultivating, and taking a gross result instead of individual ones; many shareholders in companies might receive decent dividends if one or two losing gardens were sold or leased ; as it is, they are worked on, and lessen, as a whole, the workings that would otherwise give good results. I have elsewhere noticed the wisdom of the step taken by some old companies in selling portions of their grants, when there is no possibility of their using the whole. This practice might be carried out to a still greater extent. Times in tea never seem quite bad enough to prevent some people investing —indeed, times such as those just past might almost be considered the best for capitalists. It would not be a bad plan for those who possess surplus land to put some of it into the market, and invest the proceeds in machinery : of the prudence of such a step there can be no question. Even small concerns are beginning to see this matter in its proper light ; but, unfortunately, the right kind of machine has not been invented yet—one to receive the green leaf at one end and produce dividends at the other.

I have often thought that more economy might be effected on tea estates if planters had a better insight into factory accounts before taking over charge. A manager can hardly be expected safely to economise unless he fully understands the factory books. I believe I may say that the general plan is for an assistant to know nothing whatever about keeping estate books until he is placed in charge. When the time arrives for him to submit his first accounts, he does the best he can, pro-bably with the aid of the writer, and without anyone to show him the ins and outs of the method. Or a planter, after years of work with one concern, may take service with another, and have to supply accounts on totally different forms, to study which he has no time, at all events at first; and when the end of the month comes, he has to rely on his writer, excepting, of course, as regards the cash-book. It may be said that with this book right, nothing could go far wrong; but there are unenumerated items entered in the cash-book, which cannot be properly checked at first. If planters had a more detailed knowledge of factory accounts, they would often be able to economise more than they do.

Many concerns are at the present moment working their estates with money obtained on their title-deeds. It is not long since that the confidence of Indian Banks in tea was almost shattered—at all events, it was shaken sufficiently to call in many private loans made on Tea scrip. Indian interest for loans is exorbitant, compared with the rates at which money is obtainable in England. Interest on deposits is also much higher, although not correspondingly so. Some of the Calcutta houses have had great difficulty of late in financing for tea estates, because of the critical times and the consequent want of confidence on the part of the Banks. Money might be borrowed on tea property more advantageously in London than in India. Of some loans thus effected, the actual interest has been only 2 per cent.; and even paying this in London at sterling rates has left a large margin over Indian Bank loan-rates. Estates that have been made —as, alas! many have—with borrowed money almost from the first, will require some rather skilful financing to avoid consuming their own value in interest. It has, unfortunately, been overlooked by many men able to obtain money for opening out gardens, that by the time the bushes came into bearing, three years' interest, on all accounts, would represent nearly 50 per cent. additional cost of making the estate, and a total liability be thus incurred which present prices would give but a small hope of working off. And, as I have before stated, Indian tea having found its level as to marketable value, present prices cannot be expected to increase very much. The position in which involved estates are thus placed is particularly serious; and it ought to suggest special caution to those that intend to become, or that think of becoming, working investors in Indian gardens. It was suggested to me, in writing this chapter, to go into the matter of agents' charges. To do so I should have been compelled to enter into such details as could only be given by indirectly divulging information given me in London in confidence, as to some of the Calcutta tea agencies; I am, therefore, unable to notice the subject. I would, however, just say that, to begin with, Indian Bank interest-rates are high; and agents' firms can hardly be expected to obtain money on their own security, and pass it on at the same rate to the credit of an insecure tea estate.

CHAPTER VII.

THE LABOUR QUESTION.

In 1848, the inspector of teas for the East India Company in China, after a residence of twenty-two years in the country, published a book on the cultivation and manufacture of tea. Having fully detailed every item of importance in connexion with the Chinese industry, the elaborate and valuable work closed with these words :—

" Thus, it appears, from the habits and wants of the two people—Chinese and Hindoo—from the rate of wage in the two countries, and from actual experiments, that India possesses an undoubted power of competing with China in the European and American markets in the cultivation of tea. It, therefore, only remains for the enlightened Government of Bengal, now enjoying the fruits of peace, and turning its thoughts once more to the moral and physical improvements of the people, to extend its fostering help and encouragement, as it has hitherto done, until the native population shall have

10

adopted and established the cultivation of the tea-tree
as a native product, nothing doubting that it will thereby
be administering to the comfort, happiness, and sobriety
of the people of India, as well as to increase the wealth
and commercial prosperity of the mother country and
her cherished colony."

Thus wrote Mr. Ball, more than thirty years ago ; and
looking at the tea industry of India at the present
moment, one cannot help thinking that the Government
of India is able to bear a good deal of advice without
suffering any inconvenience from it. " It only remains,"
wrote Mr. Ball, " for the *enlightened* Government of
Bengal to extend its fostering help and encouragement."
Mr. Ball is dead ; and the members of the Government of
Bengal at that time have, probably, all passed out of India,
many of them into happier (and well-deserved) spheres,
where *tálàp* is no more ; and the room that existed for
" fostering help and encouragement " has been steadily
handed down to a succession of Government officials,
and locked and closed to the real interests of the
tea-planter.   At this late period it seems well-nigh
hopeless that the thick skin of official red-tape-ism,
hardened by a long course of years, and well-barnacled
by the irritation of planters' plaints, can be pierced by
such a representation as the present one.   Yet it
is the writer's hope that—independently of Governmental acceptance of individual theories—some of the
views now put forth will lead to a clearer apprehension of the labour question by the planters and capitalists
concerned, and that an united effort may result in the

gracious extension of a small moiety of that " fostering help and encouragement of an enlightened Government " for which room exists even now more surely than when Mr. Ball first wrote the passage.

" *It only remains.*" The words meet the present state of affairs admirably. The production of Indian tea has increased from twenty pounds in 1840, to a probable fifty millions of pounds in 1881. Lakhs upon lakhs of rupees have been put into the tea industry, the merchandise of the principal Indian ports has been greatly increased thereby, hundreds of miles of deadly, unprofitable waste have been opened out, districts that were marked on maps approximately only, and by the aid of their explored boundaries, have been made habitable and valuable, hundreds of thousands of natives have been given remunerative employment, English lives and English money have been sacrificed, steamer companies, railway companies, and tramway companies have been inaugurated, to the great benefit of the country and people, posts even have been made for members of the Civil Service—and now, after forty years of work, English money, English enterprise and determination having in every branch of the great industry done everything that possibly could be done, "*it only remains for the enlightened Government of Bengal to extend its fostering help and encouragement*" to the community that is weary of waiting, *for help in respect to labour.*

It is a strange thing, this Governmental obstruction. If it were passive indifference one would not be so much surprised, because, from a tea-planter's point of view,

10 *

there is not very much that is suggestive of vigour in
the Government *Kamjari*. But the obstruction has long
taken the form of active opposition, having its source in
some remote and mystic corner which can neither be
ascertained nor assailed. Memorials and petitions to
travelling Governors-General and Lieutenant-Governors,
press representation, requests, and complaints, have
resulted, it may almost be said, only in making matters
worse. If some prominent member of the Government, of known hostility to tea-planters, had used his
power for a term of years as an obstructionist, planters
would be able to understand matters ; but Viceroys leave
India, and Lieutenant-Governors change, and tea-planters
suffer still ; the victims of bigoted prejudice, official
fallacy and shortsightedness, and the objects of a continuous unfairness which seems to be handed down from
régime to *régime*, and to be kept as actively hostile as was
the oppression of the children of Israel through a
succession of Pharaohs who knew not Joseph

I hope I shall be able to establish my case, that this
want of countenance on the part of the Government is
fallacious and shortsighted. But before so doing, it
ought to be mentioned that planters are not unmindful
of their mercies. Many of them see a Bishop once in
two or three years ; there are *dák* bungalows in some
districts, put up for planters and used by road-engineers
and forest *daragohs* ; planters can obtain their letters
from the post-offices by sending their own men for
them ; their lives are cheered half-yearly by receiving a
great bundle of forms, bearing testimony to the tabula-

tory skill of some of the Government officials who have never been in the tea districts ; at about the same interval Government sends round an Inspector to see that the coolies are treating their Sahib properly. Government also sometimes opens its heart, and gives a planter Rs. 100 to repair a road used by the public, and which annually costs Rs. 500 to keep in order. Then there are Assistant and Deputy Commissioners who, being up to the last thing in Jurisprudence, will fine a cooly four annas for flatly refusing to do a day's work, and, through the medium of a printed invite, will ask the planter-employer to go into court to witness the majesty of the law; by which the said planter possibly has a ride of thirty or more miles, loses the labour of several witnesses, and, likely enough, is away from his factory at the time when he could least be spared. And then there is a police-service—incorruptible and un-defiled—composed of men who are always quite ready to arrest purloiners of factory property, if the Sahib will show where the culprits are.*

* I remember two cases in Cachar. A planter had some boats stolen from his *ghát*. He used his best efforts to obtain *Khábár* of them, but failing, sent a full report to the Police Superintendent. The official answer came that the robbers should assuredly be arrested, and the boats returned, if the planter would send word as to their exact location. Case 2.—Another planter sent a man into the station with Rs. 100 in silver to exchange for notes with the garden agent. As coolies went, this was a trustworthy man. But as he did not return at the proper time, inquiries were made, but without avail, so full particulars as to the man's appear-ance, &c. were sent to the Silchar Police Superintendent. Two days later, a constable arrived at the factory, with an official

Such are some of brighter phases of the fostering help
and encouragement of an enlightened Government. The
only explanation I know of having ever been advanced
as to the relentless opposition before mentioned, is
explained in that stereotyped and undying cry—" the
Brutal Planter." It has been sounded and maintained
in India by people who were in English nurseries at the
time that the Indian press gave the preliminary howl ;
the howl, strange to say, that has been applied to the
various communities of planters all the world over—
West Indian, South American, Tirhoot, Wynaad. Well-
meaning-people in Calcutta have expressed a hope to
me that tea-planters were not so cruel as they were
generally believed to be ; and precisely the same thing
has been said to me in England. In 1875 a native
playwright took up the old strain in Calcutta, and brought
out ·" *Chá ka Durpán Náták* "—a mirror that revealed
about as much truth regarding factory *dástoor*, as, I
suppose, the writer's own glass did beauty when he looked
into it. Because, many years ago, a few isolated cases
of ill-treatment came before the public notice in India,
tea-planters have ever since been stamped with the mark
of the beast, and officially looked upon almost in the
light of *quasi*-slave-drivers, from whom coolies had to

application for particulars. (They had all been given before.) Four
days later, a notification was received that if the manager would
send word where the man was, he would be arrested at once. I
believe, in replying, the planter thanked the Superintendent, and
said that were he cognizant of the individual's whereabouts, he
would undertake to arrest him himself, and, perhaps, with the aid
of a big stick, persuade him to return to the factory.

be protected with the utmost vigilance. At least, this is the only explanation I have been able to obtain, and the information was given me by a magistrate who had long resided in Assam, and who was well up in all matters relating to the tea industry. The gross injustice of judging, after the lapse of a number of years, the gentlemen now representing the planting communities, upon a conclusion arrived at when the fraternity consisted of an utter medley of Europeans and Eurasians, is patent to anyone possessing even a moderate knowledge of the ways of tea-planters. I take it on the authority of past writers and official inquiries, that at one period the people allowed to pass the Government agents as fit for working on tea estates, were, some of them, ex-mutineers, offshoots of the great Barabbas family, town coolies, and the dregs and " riff-raff " of bazaars situated far from good recruiting-grounds. It is no cause for wonder, either that such men refused to do the work set them, or that the planter—believing the men able to work because they had been passed by the Government official—was sometimes resolute in the interest of his estate. I would ask the Indian readers of this book, just for a moment to remember the groups of coolies they may have seen in Calcutta, particularly in the vicinity of the markets in the early mornings, and at the street corners with their baskets later on, and inquire whether it was right for such men to be passed up as fit for the tea districts, to fell timber or to hoe in the sun or rain ? Had the Government been honestly anxious to protect cooly emigrants, they could have done so in one move—by refusing to pass such men as were physically unfit for the work they agreed to do. To pass them, and then cry out at what was bound to be the sequel, was grossly unjust. Such men were allowed to go to the factories; and the consequence was that in many cases planters found themselves surrounded by a number of totally useless coolies, skilled, some of them, in the art of rebellion, deceived, all of them, by the official passing them as fit for the life before them; and, by degrees, constant warfare resulted, in which the coolies sought to beat the Sahib, and the Sahib, seeing the odds against him, strove to maintain his position and to get his work done, by such means as were at hand. I write advisedly on this subject, after very careful inquiries and correspondence with old tea-planters now in England, and not merely to prove that the social phases of tea-planting have now all changed, nor metaphorically to rub down the community of which, until recently, I was a member. No reflexion whatever is made on the old tea-planters; as but for them, the present ones might have been badly off; but it is a proved state of things, not at all confined to the Indian Tea industry, that there is always a certain amount of rough treatment for some section of a community that comes suddenly into existence in a new field of speculation. If the field be genuine, the speculative phase will pass off in the course of years, and the industry become one of steady investment; the rough element in it will also move elsewhere, and law-abiding men form the fraternity. Look, for instance, at the antecedents of the very first Australian squatters, and at the class of men now holding cattle-runs. Look, also, at the Kimberly Diamond fields; the knife, revolver, and tent element has passed away, small claims have been taken up by companies, and the Kimberly fields, according to South African papers, now represent a highly respectable township with a mayor and corporation, and are the working seats of several companies, as sound in their holdings as some of the best Indian Tea gardens. In past days the suffering, roughing it, and sickness were not confined to the natives on tea estates. There are graves in the different districts which could tell harrowing tales of European life struggling against a deadly climate, and of surroundings that were infinitely worse for the white than for the black man. The latter could get the food of his own country at all events, but the former could not; the cooly had a house that was as good as any he had been used to, but the European had not. When the black was sick he was attended to and treated beneficially, as far as lay in the planter's power, and as he had never been in his own home; but as a rule, when the Sahib was sick, though it were unto death, there was no one to attend *to him*. Scanty food of an everlasting sameness; no liquor as a regular thing; bad health; bad house; bad servants. The Government and the press cried out about the misery of the black man, and in the characteristic mode of Anglo-Saxon philanthropy, forgot all about the white man, who was suffering a great deal more. That there were some cases of gross ill-treatment and unfairness, cannot be denied, and I do not wish to account for them by the then unpleasantnesses or the associations or the planter's life. They were isolated, separate, and distinct. But then there is hardly a community in the world that at no period of its history has had the misfortune to record some occurrence or other that was disgraceful and frequently brutal. It is very great nonsense at this late date—and in the total absence of any confirmatory evidence whatever that a similarity now exists between the past and present state of things—to continue to stigmatise the planter as "brutal," or to act in keeping with the supposition, when not a working day in any year can now be found to pass in England without the press recording at least one case of atrocious, shocking brutality, in which, generally, a woman is the victim. The belief still persistently upheld in many parts of India and in England, that because, years ago, the employers of large bodies of labourers were found to ill-treat the blacks, the same state of things must continue now, is logically unsound; and the inference drawn by the Government that, as planters are not to be trusted, labourers must be practically discouraged or even prevented from emigrating at will to the tea districts, is logically unfair.

But I say emphatically, that things have changed for both Europeans and natives, and changed for the better; because the speculative craze has exhausted itself, and people put their money in, and settle down to, Indian

tea, as a safe and sound investment, that will give a
good return in exchange for careful management, knowledge, and hard work. Because of this, labour has become infinitely too valuable to be treated badly. Good
coolies are far too difficult to obtain to be ill-treated or
crossed when secured. *Labour is the great machinery by
which tea-land is made valuable* ; and it is costly machinery,
too, especially for Assam tea-planters. Now, no man
would be fool enough to buy a machine, and then
wilfully damage it ; and precisely the same thing may
be said of tea-planters in regard to their labour. Putting
aside all moral considerations (which in many cases have
great weight), there are many solid reasons for which a
planter would refrain from treating his labourer badly.
There are gardens, in every district, which are always open
to run-away or time-expired coolies. At present the
maximum term of cooly service is three years ; and
it requires no great effort on the part of a native to
remember injustice or severity during that period, and so
to refuse to renew his agreement when it expires. Now,
it costs nearly Rs. 100 to get a good jungly cooly from
Bengal to Assam (I know of cases where the cost was
much higher). Distributed over the three years of
service, Rs. 33.5.4 per head per annum, or Rs. 2.12.5
per mensem, is represented. Now, say a planter in one
year gets up fifty such coolies. In addition to whatever
pay they may earn, the annual blanket, and the sale of
rice at a probable loss, for three years there is represented on account of these coolies Rs. 138.14.2 per
mensem, or Rs. 1,666.10.8 per annum, besides the

cost of houses, medicine, and hospital comforts, which
give no tangible results, and can benefit no one save the
individual cooly himself, nor be recovered from anyone.
It would be, I should imagine, impossible to arrive at
the exact value of a cooly's labour in its relation to the
amount of tea or profit made on the whole workings of
a year ; but with this heavy debit running through the
first three years, it may safely be said that, useful as it
is, there is not a great deal of profit on the labour given
in the first term of service. It is after this, when the
cooly and the Sahib know each other, and the man has
become acclimatized, that his real value begins ; and it
is only by sheer diplomacy, unless there are strong
family reasons for his remaining, that the planter can
retain his cooly. There are gardens that will give a
large proportion of the cost of importation as a bonus to
a good cooly for a three years' agreement ; the manager
reasoning, very logically, that it is far more economical
to get a three years' contract from an acclimatised man
for, say, Rs. 50, than to pay Rs. 100 for a new one from
Bengal. As to whether it is neighbourly so to do, will
be considered afterwards. It must be acknowledged
that sometimes when a cooly has been for three years on
a factory, he naturally enough thinks he would like a
change ; and should it happen that the manager has not
come up to his notion of what a Sahib ought to be,
nothing save his relationships will induce him to remain.
Old sirdars (at the Sahib's *hookum*) may coax and cajole
as the *hubble-bubble* passes round at night ; but the verbal
hikmát is insufficient. The manager may expatiate upon

the advantages of the factory, the good water and hospital, and villages and bazaars near at hand, the small number of deaths, and the cleanliness of the garden, "which is not like some of these new *bágichás*, always getting into jungle, and making work very heavy for the coolies," &c. &c. &c. ; but it will be of no avail —there will be the regulation answer that a *bhai* at another factory wants the individual, and he must go to him.

It is almost useless to endeavour to reason with coolies. If they fancy they have cause to dislike the Sahib on the factory, nothing will remove the idea, and even a large bonus will not prevail upon them to stop. I have been occasionally unable to help thinking that agents did not seem to be *fully* aware of the almost primary importance and great value of a manager who got on well with his labour ; and I think this lack of just estimation is the outcome of the ignorance of the management of coolies, which residents in towns cannot be expected to have an intimate knowledge of. Every planter knows well enough that the most detrimental thing that can happen to him is to get a bad name amongst coolies ; and the matter cuts the other way, too, for the best qualification a manager can have is that of being successful with his labourers. It is not of much use for one to be able to make good tea, if the tea-house hands are constantly changing through men leaving. I have written more fully on this subject of cooly-management in another chapter, and it is here only necessary to notice the abstract result. No matter

what the causes may be, a planter is invariably considered inefficient if his labourers go away in any
numbers—excepting, perhaps, in the cases of minor
assistants, who are responsible to resident managers ;
and then it may happen that the *Burra Sahib*, understanding matters, exonerates his assistant, and draws
the blame on himself.   Of course, it is not for a moment
to be wondered at that information as to unrenewed
agreements is most unpalatable to estate agents.   If
" nothing succeeds like success," it is equally certain
that nothing fails like failure.   When a garden is doing
badly, and coolies leave, and the manager writes that
he must have more labour, even to keep the garden
out of jungle, the agents have good reason to ex-
claim : " Ah ! it never rains but it pours.   Here is
Loksán Barree already on the wrong side of the books,
and now the labour is leaving ! "   And they would most
probably think the manager had better be changed, in
which case the planter's prospect would be very bad—
going from a garden that did not pay, because he could
not keep his labour.   This would be failure indeed.   Even
when a manager is doing well, and seems to be in swing-
ing prosperity, he may be suddenly very seriously in-
convenienced by a number of cooly agreements running
out, and his progress thwarted by insufficient labour to
maintain the momentum.   It is easy enough to understand how, in either of these cases, the planter would
strive his utmost to retain his coolies, and unpleasant as
it would be for him to report failure to Calcutta, it surely
would not be less unpleasant for his agents to receive

the information. What I wish particularly to point out is, that knowing he can look only to himself for success with his labourers, and knowing, too, that failure with them will stamp him both locally and in Calcutta as inefficient, every manager is absolutely compelled, *in his own interest*, to leave no stone unturned to ensure success with his coolies. Planters have to manage their labourers with an eye to the future, and not to act arbitrarily during the course of an agreement, because, once in a while, at all events, the usual relations of planter and cooly are reversed, and that is when the former asks the latter to renew—because the latter never, or hardly ever, goes to the former to ask that he may be allowed to do so. A young assistant, recently out from home, may very likely have a notion that coolies are not of much account; but before he obtains his first charge, he will (or ought to) have found out that in many matters it is necessary, for his own sake, to be thick-skinned with coolies, because they are of far greater value and importance than might be thought when they commence a conversation with "*Ap ka gholám*." Coolies' interests are identical with the personal ones of the planter; and because of this it may be said without any hesitation that coolies are treated well. Importing a number of them, of course, lessens the garden profit, and with it the manager's commission. Inability to retain his labourers must eventually result in a planter being replaced. The value of a manager who gets on well with his labour, is of no visionary kind. Local superintendents and divisional managers of concerns are always ready

enough to get a good man to their side if they can.
I remember one case where Rs. 50 per mensem
was refused ; the planter resigned, and before he gave
up charge of his factory, was appointed to another
one near at hand ; twenty-five old coolies followed
him to his new quarters in a few weeks, and the agents
who had refused him Rs. 600 per annum, had to re-
place these coolies, in new unacclimatised men, at the
cost of the difference between the bonus to the old ones,
and that of importing fresh ones, or about Rs. 70 per
head, or for twenty-five adults Rs. 1,750, when they
could have kept the manager for Rs. 600.   It was said
at the time that even then the agents gained, because
three years of the manager's increase would have been
Rs. 1,800—Rs. 50 more than the cost of the coolies ;
but subsequent events drove this idea out of reckoning,
as the twenty-five coolies were but the first instalments
of others who followed as their agreements expired.
This will show *the value* of a planter who manages his
labourers successfully.   Perhaps some will say that it
was very wrong and malicious of the planter to take the
coolies. 1 cannot see it.   But his good reputation
amongst natives had been used for his garden's benefit
in past times, and as he could not himself take a fresh
charge and transfer his reputation to his successor,
he took it with him for the interests of his new
employers, as he would have kept it for his old ones, had
they been more generously inclined.

Therefore, for the reasons here given, I hope I have
made it clear that the planter's interests are combined

with the cooly's well-being and contentment; and I consequently think it quite unnecessary to endeavour further to prove that the planter is treating himself badly in treating his cooly badly, that he fully understands this, and is not ass enough to do it.

I am anxious to construct this chapter as follows :—

I.—To show the importance of the tea industry and planters' work generally, and the labour requirements ;

II.—To show the only known cause of the absence of Governmental countenance to the same ;

III.—To show the fallacy of such cause, as being contrary to the planter's own interest ;

IV.—To show what is the real state of affairs on tea estates ;

V.—To show how Government might help the planter in respect to labour ; and how, in thus doing, Government would help the revenues and peoples of India at large ;

Together with one or two observations which may help planters and agents to see their own side of the labour question in a clearer light.

It may seem rather odd to give a skeleton of this chapter when half the questions to be noticed are written upon ; but the subject is proving of greater length than I anticipated, and long chapters without distinct sections are apt to be confusing.

Governing coolies is not always a jovial occupation. In the planter's position with his labour-staff there is much to irritate, provoke, and sadden. As I have said

11

before, it is well-nigh impossible to *reason* with coolies, and they are naturally very obstinate through their ignorance. I cannot uphold the opinion often expressed in India that the cooly is totally devoid of the power of feeling grateful. I know there is very much—I have myself experienced it—to lead to this belief; but I have found exceptions to it. Where a planter is blessed with an accurate conception of his duty, and acts upon it, there will be some of his coolies who will grow to like him, and who will be liked by him in return; and, so far as work goes, there will also be developed a feeling of perfect trust. It is this way of thinking and working continually that establishes the planter's position on his factory, and makes the coolies ready to follow him should he leave, and the Sahib to want the coolies in the same event. And there is much to bring about this oneness of feeling, especially in the case of a new garden. For then the coolies are comfortably housed before the Sahib, who is most likely to be in a lonely spot at some distance from European neighbours; and as the time passes, he sees his patch of clearing increasing by acres, his nurseries thriving, his cooly-lines multiplying, and his sick-list growing less. In the evening when his work is done, having no better society, he saunters down to the cooly-lines and chats with the people, who also are resting after the work of the day. They look to him for everything. He gets rice for them, has a shop established, plans their houses, and often, as an inducement to stay, lends them money to buy cows, and purchases the milk for himself and the hospital, treats them

when they are sick, and feels their value. He explains
his plans to the sirdars, pointing out the land he intends
to clear, the site of the bungalow, &c.; he is out with the
men all day, knows their worth, and the name of each.
In the case of old gardens, coolies are particularly well-
off. Planters are at all times most anxious to have
their lines put up in healthy places, and numbers
of houses have been abandoned at the doctor's suggestion, for the benefit of the coolies' health. Houses
are built on high land, plastered inside and out, well
thatched and drained, and men told off to the duty of
keeping the lines quite clean. Every morning all sick
labourers can go to the doctor, or, if there is no such
officer, to the planter, to be treated; and I may say,
without fear of contradiction, that men who are really
unwell are never sent to work. (Some lazy ones often
pretend to be sick, and are sent about their business.)
Whenever a man feels unwell in the course of his work
he is always at liberty to leave off and go to the doctor,
and then to his own house. Or if he be quite laid by,
and can earn no money, he goes to the hospital and is
fed and treated. In this respect he is far better off
than his master. Planters' fare is painfully regular; and
the diet during sickness is necessarily the same as in
health, excepting, perhaps, that some tinned delicacies
are indulged in. But when coolies are sick, they are
given soup, corn-flour, arrowroot, and tea, and whatever
can be provided for them is freely procured; and they
stand a better chance of regaining their health and suffering no ill after-effects than the European, who has no

11

one to see that he takes his medicine and attends to himself; if he knows what to do, in the depressing effects of fever, he frequently does not do it; and he goes on in a condition of indifferent health, trusting to chance to pull through. But the cooly is attended to regularly, and gets well quickly. When convalescent, he is put to light work; but for the planter, ill or well, the duties remain unchanged. In the case of new coolies, generally, on arrival, a quantity of rice and other diet is given them; they are allowed a day or two to settle down and make companionships, are then put on whatever work is most pressing, and paid in full, irrespective of the amount of work done. At least, such has been my experience. In this way, drawing full pay for some time, they are able to get the necessary cooking utensils a good cloth or two, &c., and to make themselves cosy. If they are put on hoeing, they are paid full wages, because their hands are always too soft at first to do the full task. The majority of coolies on the majority of estates, are well satisfied with their lot, and it would be difficult to say what more could be given them than they already receive. Great care is taken to ensure a supply of good water; vegetable gardens are made in odd corners, cow-houses are built, and shelter put up for goats; pigs grunt about the lines and drive away the snakes, and the coolies are peaceful and contented. It is quite a pleasant sight, when the day's work is done, to sit in one's verandah and look toward the cooly lines. Slowly the smoke of many fires ascends into the air; outside the houses, during the hot weather, groups of coolies are to be seen sitting round the family fire, the men smoking and gossiping, and the women preparing the evening meal. The cows have been driven in from the pastures (the herds being provided by the factory), the goats have been penned and the day's work measured ; and here the people sit waiting for their repast. It is ready at length ; and although the modes of serving and despatch are primeval rather than elegant, a happy, contented spirit reigns throughout the lines. Later in the evening the *tom-tom* sounds ; men chaunt, and women dance ; perhaps there is a big dinner on a small scale at the house of a sirdar, or given by a father on the birth of a son, and, when carried on in moderation, the sounds of simple festivity rise pleasantly in the evening air. And the Sahib, while not envying the coolies their surroundings, feels that they are enjoying the society of their fellows, and need nothing more than they possess ; and it is not unlikely that he will think of, and realise, his isolated position, in which reading and smoking after dinner are (or, as they go jointly, is) the only occupation he can indulge in ; and he probably turns into his bedroom, and under his mosquito-net, with that strange feeling on him which looking out into the silence of night seems to bring to all planters at some time or other, but which cannot be described. There can be no doubt that natives appreciate the state of affairs brought about for them by the majority of garden managers ; and this is strikingly proved where there happen to be native-managed gardens near those under European supervision. Two gardens, which I knew when they were owned and worked by native managers, were hardly ever out of jungle; and many of the flushes that managed to come were lost, because hardly any local labour could be induced to work. Oddly enough, both of these gardens (in different districts) were little flat patches, and the European-managed ones near at hand, to which local labour readily went, were hilly. I thought that, perhaps. money was uncertain ; but found, on inquiries, this was not the case, but that simply the natives liked the Sahib's *bágichás* best.

Government officials often wish it to be thought that they have a lively sense of the probable sufferings of the cooly. Surely planters suffer too ! Mental discomfort, such as coolies cannot understand ; physical discomfort from the extreme climate ; social discomfort in the greatest degree ; and when they are sick, their strong constitutions and muscular bodies offer far more substance for fever to play on than does the cooly physique. Fortunately, a far more satisfactory state of affairs now exists in regard to medical attendance than was the case some years ago. Medical assistants in many cases have been added to the factory staff, and native doctors, it may almost be said, are numerous—acting, generally, under the supervision of a European medical officer, who visits them weekly or fortnightly, and who is always available in urgent cases. But such cases are very rare ; cooly complaints being generally represented by a few simple diseases that can easily be treated successfully.

With so much in his favour, no wonder the cooly is contented, and follows his Sahib when he believes him to be the source of his comfort. I am here reminded of an instance in Cachar, where a planter had a batch of thirty Madrassi coolies sent him, who were very feeble and faint-hearted. Every morning before going to work, they were taken to the hospital, and each man was given something more than a spoonful of rum and milk. This treatment was continued for weeks, with the most beneficial results. At another place, in the rainy season, when men started working very early in the morning, the manager was surprised to find bowel complaints largely on the increase. He instituted inquiries, examined the wells, &c. without success; but at last ascertained the cause. Many of the coolies had got into the way every evening of cooking sufficient rice for the then meal, and also for the early morning one, which latter they ate cold. In standing over several hours after boiling, the rice fermented and was very injurious as food. So the manager forbade this being done any more, explained matters to the coolies, rang them up at the usual time in the morning, but gave them an hour after the first gong to cook their rice and have their meal properly.

On some Assam gardens I know well, the Kachari coolies often finished their day's work of hoeing by nine o'clock in the morning; and Bengalis (who, as a class, rise later), by ten or eleven o'clock. They had then the rest of the day to themselves, or could go out and work "ticca." Some of them would thus do three days' work in one. Can any "overtime" such as this be found in England?

Planters grow to take a very keen interest in their coolies, knowing whom they marry, and often the names of their children, and. always doing their utmost to relieve them in times of sickness. I remember one Christmas, when there was a Cholera epidemic in the district, the annual dinner in the station showed several vacant chairs, where planters from outside factories felt too saddened to join the festivities, because of the fearful scourge then raging. Let a man who has an unfavourable opinion of tea-planters be with any one of them during a visitation of Cholera, and he will never again talk about the "brutal" planter. Rather, if he has not been used to treating blacks, he will admire the courage and kindness which are drawn from the heart of every planter when his coolies are afflicted with this terrible curse.

It is a cooly's own fault if he is not happy. But, having given the bright side of native life on tea estates, I am going to give an equally truthful dark one. Unfortunately, dissatisfied members are to be found in every community of men or women ; and in the tea districts these folk cause much that is undesirable in the planter's life. The first and greatest cause of these unpleasantnesses is that unsuitable coolies are sent up. On one occasion I was visiting at a factory when a batch of new coolies arrived. The planter inquired of each what had been his work in his own country ; and one tall angular youth said that he had earned his bread by rubbing oil into a fat old Baboo ! Fancy sending such a man to hoe a tea-garden ! Of course, had this lad been one of an otherwise agricultural family who were all going up, there would have been nothing to say, for planters are always glad to see relatives keeping together; but, as it was, the lad was without relations. In the case of depôt coolies, it is to be regretted that very often gross misrepresentations are made; and where a man's caste would cause him to be rejected as unsuitable, this is changed in the lists provided, and the planter is misled. Really healthy coolies are not often troublesome. The sickly ones, or those who indulge in *bháng* or *gánja*, are generally the fractious individuals, and these are constantly getting into hot water, quarrelling, working badly, or possibly flatly refusing to work at all. Now, it is maintained as being contrary to law for any unauthorised individual to act as is only in the power of the court to order; and planters have frequently been told in court, that when a man refuses to work, the right thing is to charge him in court with breach of contract. I once was so pleasantly situated, that the nearest court on one side of me was sixty-five miles off, and on the other about forty-five. On first taking my overcharge, one or two cases occurred, of men flatly refusing to go to the work to which they were told off. This question being a rather delicate one, I purposely give my own experience. Now I had been given my charge on the supposition that I could get my work done, and at first there was a good deal of it to do. I should like to know whether any man who has had to manage blacks would say I acted sensibly if I had gone through the official routine of charging these men with

breach of contract.   Say I made but one journey to the
nearest court, I should have had ninety miles to travel ;
witnesses would have been necessary, and they would
have taken at the very least four days for the double
journey, beside their time in court ; my coolies would
have known that they could openly defy me, and put me
to the trouble of going backward and forward to court ;
and the result of their deliberate refusal to work, my
wasted time, and the witnesses' lost labour, would have
been—What ?   That which I have known to be pronounced in court as the reading of the law on the
subject—*a fine of four annas for the day of refusal, and a
like sum for each day's absence in the case!*   My coolies
were not fined at all, and they did their work.   By the
way, it occurs to me in writing, that boys are birched at
school for disobedience, and soldiers are punished with
the cat for the same offence sometimes.   Supposing the
latter to be authorised, what *legalises* the former—
necessity ?

If laws of no possible utility are made, planters
must supplement them by others which have a more
practical bearing on the case.   Legal authority, as set
forth in punishment, is supposed to reform ; but no
lazy cooly could be even improved by a four-annas fine
—especially when he knew that to get that imposed the
factory had lost a larger number of rupees.   The experience of some Bengali coolies in Assam has been
that offending against the law is a very advantageous
proceeding.   Coolies return from some of the jails in
far better condition than they have ever been before.

The only disgrace is that they have to wear a uniform *dhoti*, and when put on to hoe ground, weed or make roads, they are presided over by a Sepoy armed with a shooting-iron, which I have myself seen placed under a tree to guard the Sepoy as he slept, and (presumably) to impress upon the prisoners the *awfulness of crime*— as they squatted and chatted at their perfect ease. Then, soon after, the day's work being done, they returned to their temporary residence to have their evening meal. This is the punishment for much more serious offences than merely refusing to work.

Occasionally events transpire in connection with labour that are almost disastrous to the planter. It is bad enough when agreements expire, and coolies will not renew them; but it is by no means a rare thing for a batch of new coolies, after being a few days on an estate, to clear out (or literally, bolt), leaving no trace behind them. The only thing that a planter can do is to write a circular-letter, and send it round to all the neighbouring factories, asking permission for the bearers to search for the runaways. This is always given, and the planter writes " seen "; but it is seldom indeed that the absconders are found. I remember, when in Assam, a notice of this kind reached me, stating that a batch of thirteen new coolies had levanted after being one night in the factory. Here was a loss of over a thousand rupees; and I afterwards learnt that none of the people had been found. This kind of thing is positively grievous to planters. I have previously mentioned the police. Now in England, if a man (or men) absconded with valuables to the amount of a hundred pounds, almost every police-station in the kingdom would be apprized of the fact, and a notice of the same posted up. But in the tea-districts there is nothing of this kind ; and the law which is so ready to fine a planter for using force to make a man do the work he has contracted to do, gives no aid whatever when the planter's money is going out like this. In cases such as these, the planter is generally considered at fault ; and really, this is not to be wondered at. Yet what is he to do ? The coolies arrive as other batches have arrived, they are housed and fed ; and perhaps at daybreak, a few mornings after, word is brought that they have gone. Coolies cannot be padlocked in their houses like cattle. Very likely several roads lead from the factory, and the planter sends messengers on each   He can do no more. If there are any police near, they are of no use; and information has to be sent to Calcutta, which is as unsatisfactory as it would be to say that so many hundreds of rupees had been thrown into a river. This kind of thing must naturally affect all concerned. Planters almost fear to trust their coolies, and agents think there must be something radically wrong for people to abscond like this and not be recovered ; so the manager gets discredit and discomfort both ways.

It often leaks out by degrees, after coolies have gone, that men from other estates have been in the lines, for purposes which could not be explained. In most factories it is the custom for a report to be made to the manager every evening as to absent coolies and visiting ones in the lines. But it is easy enough for an outside man to say he has come from a near factory to visit his friends, and it can hardly be proved that he has not. No planter can prevent the public passing through his garden, provided they go in an orderly manner. But, often enough, these men " from near factories " come from distant gardens to ascertain as to expiring agreements, and to persuade coolies to leave ; and natives will sometimes be thus induced to go to estates scores of miles off. It is hardly necessary to say that for one planter to poach upon another's labour is most unfair. A man's position is often entirely dependent upon his successful management and retention of his coolies ; and, unfortunately, it must be acknowledged that cases occur in which natives are persuaded to leave a factory before their agreements expire. There can be no term for this other than robbery ; and it is a very aggravated kind of robbery, too, because it takes away that which cannot be immediately replaced, and on which very much is dependent. In briefly noticing this subject in my former pamphlet, I said that I was glad to know that an Association was in course of formation to protect planters from this kind of thing. From information afterwards obtained, I believe the scheme fell through completely. It is useless to try to call this taking away agreement labour by a milder term than has been used ; but justice compels me to look on all sides of the question. Many gardens are in such financial difficulties that agents cannot send up coolies ; yet managers know that unless they obtain a certain result notwithstanding, they will have to go. While dishonesty can never be recommended as an admissible means to an end, I must confess that it is difficult to say what course is open to the planter. And although not always, he is sometimes to be exonerated from the charge of dishonesty, as on the representations of his (local) recruiters, he is led to believe that the coolies he may soon expect are all time-expired people. It has been tried in some districts to organise a system among planters by which no coolies would be engaged locally excepting on showing a certificate of discharge. But there are always managers who cannot agree to this. They say that they are short of labour, and must get all they can ; and if a new man present himself as a time-expired cooly from elsewhere, he will be taken gladly. When we remember what worry, anxiety, and seemingly hopeless struggling insufficient labour means for the planter, it gives no cause for surprise that short-handed men should thus act. I hope to show further on how all this might be avoided if Government would aid the planter. Another irritation to garden-managers is caused by men—not a few in number—who go the round of districts, asking to be put on agreement and receiving the bonus, working for a few days or weeks, and then levanting, going to another factory under a different name and performing the same round, and so on, until they are caught. The following was an experience of my own. I was working a new garden, which was very short of labour. A man presented himself, and asked for a year's agreement, saying he came from a factory about twenty miles off where he had served for three years. Not being able to explain satisfactorily why he wished to come to my factory, I said he might work if he liked, but I should not put him under agreement until he had been some time on the place. He remained for about three weeks, and worked well; and I then put him on a one-year's contract. He went on for about two months more, when I received a letter from a planter at some distance, whom I had not the pleasure of knowing, saying that it was reported to him that a man who had taken a year's agreement at his factory, and levanted soon after, was under agreement to me—would I allow his messengers to search in my lines? I knew that no such-named man was on my books, but the men made inquiries, and said they could ascertain nothing. Soon after, my new agreement wallah absconded, and I unsuccessfully tried to find him. An old sirdar told me a little while later, that he believed the man was constantly coming into the factory at night, trying to persuade some of the coolies to abscond. I offered, through the sirdar, a reward for the man's apprehension. When some of my coolies were at a neighbouring bazaar shortly after, my absconder was seen, and—well, he was brought back to me. As a runaway agreement-cooly, I placed him in durance vile, and sent in an application to the police-superintendent that he might be formally arrested on the double charge of absconding when under agreement, and for endeavouring to entice away other agreement-coolies. While waiting the result, the planter who had written me before, again wrote saying that further information led him to believe that his man was in my factory, passing under the name used by my lately-captured agreement-wallah. This individual was interviewed by the bearers of the letter, and identified. Eventually, he was sentenced to imprisonment on the double charge, and I believe that as soon as he left the jail free on my account, he was arrested on a similar indictment instituted by the planter referred to. It transpired that this man was a regular recruiting agent for some gardens nearly a hundred miles away; that his plan was to give a year's agreement at a factory, spend his money freely amongst the coolies, and then persuade them to follow him to the planters who employed him, and by whom, of course, he was well paid. But it is as likely as not that all men so taken were represented as time-expired people.

I said, in an earlier part of this chapter, that governing coolies was not a jovial occupation, and I hope I have explained some of the causes of this being the case. When coolies abide by their contracts, they make the Sahib's life easy, and are themselves well-cared for, kindly treated, and enjoy an existence that is a perfect Elysium to what is the order of things in their own country. Coolies who behave themselves and do their work want for nothing and save money; and I know of one case where a man deposited sixty rupees with his Sahib as a guarantee that he would return to the factory after visiting his home. His agreement was out, and he was at liberty to leave finally; but he lodged this money of his own free will as an assurance that he would return, and he considerably augmented it with the bonus for a three-years' agreement, when he did so. The act was good testimony as to whether coolies who do their work are badly treated. There are troublesome, vicious, evil-disposed men on tea estates, who harass the planter's life more than can be described; and there are good, steady, reliable men, who thoroughly believe in the Sahib and his *dástoor*. But both classes receive equally such consideration and kind treatment as is in the planter's power to give; and where any suffer at all, it is because they will persist in being obstinate, instead of following the example of their fellows, to whom life is thoroughly enjoyable.

The great machinery upon which all industries are dependent, is labour. In speaking to an Official some time since on the reluctance of the Government to help tea-planters, I was told that, as a community, they were never satisfied, even though laws had been passed which enabled almost any man to take up land. I admitted that the last land laws of Assam and Cachar were certainly favourable; but that it was not a very gigantic piece of generosity to give to planters land that no one else would use, and which, in being utilised, benefited the country immensely. And I (perhaps naturally) asked what was the use of the Goverment making laws by which any man could take up land, when, by the action of the same Government, it was so difficult to obtain labour to develop its value? It was equivalent to asking men to make bricks without straw. I told the Official that I knew of miles upon miles of excellent tea-land in Central Assam, along the Government road, running parallel with a river leading directly into the Brahmapootra, and navigable all the year round, but in which district, during a several hours' elephant journey, no village, or even hut, was to be seen, excepting the roadside bungalows, erected at intervals by and for the road engineer The neighbourhood was simply and absolutely devoid of any inhabitants, excepting in the hills near at hand. In the spot to which I refer, if labour were brought up in the usual course from Bengal, the tea industry might be increased immensely, without the fear of planters squabbling over land. The road and river communication is simply magnificent ; and if a giant Company could be formed to take up this district, it would, I am sure, meet with certain success. Manufacturing could be centralised in a manner that I have never else-where seen such advantages for. Planters would at first have to colonise the place, and look to themselves for everything ; but after a while the Assamese might be attracted and villages made, in which poultry would be procurable. Planters have done this kind of thing before. At one time I had occasion to consider the preliminaries for starting a garden in the district, and I found that a satisfactory commencement could be made with the hill-labour near at hand. I recently learned that the land remains unopened. Now, this is but one of many such spots, in which remunerative occupation could be provided for innumerable natives, if they were more easily procurable. A few pages back I endeavoured to give an accurate statement as to the condition of Bengali coolies on tea estates in Assam and Cachar, in the section of this chapter, " To show what is the real state of affairs on tea estates." Now the reluctance of the Government to help planters with labour might reasonably be supposed to indicate a condition of contentment and prosperity in the districts used by planters as recruiting grounds, by reason of which it is a positive unkindness to endeavour to persuade natives to leave their homes for the tea districts. The closing section of this chapter will unavoidably be a long one. It is " To show how Government might help the planter in respect to labour, and how, in thus doing, Government would be helping the revenues and the peoples of India at large."

It will be admitted, readily enough, that where land has been lying waste from time immemorial, there would have been nothing to encourage vegetarian settlers to it, who were unable to obtain a living on it. Thus it has been with many of the tea districts; high land being unsuitable for rice cultivation, natives have passed it by, and peopled spots more suitable to their own needs. The population of these spots has been increased only in the small ratio of family additions, and not by any large influx of enterprising cultivators. Therefore, local labour has been totally inadequate for the tea enterprise. Thus the planter's need has arisen ; and he has looked to the populous districts of Bengal for help. If the places to which he so looked were able to provide satisfactorily for their inhabitants, Government would have been justified in letting the planter fight his own way in prevailing on natives to leave their holdings. But if, on the other

12 *

hand, such places were totally unable to provide for their population, and if the people themselves were in the very lowest depths of degraded, helpless, awful poverty, ground down by taxation which has resulted from ignorance, and mortgaged, well-nigh body and soul, to local money-lenders—if, I say, the people whom planters wanted, lived by chronic starvation that is heart-rending to know of, because their rulers could not understand their needs, or, understanding, would not recognise them and ameliorate their terrible misery—then, I say, in such a case, every man of even *minimum* intelligence would suppose that a professedly Christian Government would be sincerely glad of any opportunity whatever for improving the condition of such people. And I say, too, that this latter is the actual condition of the majority of Bengal *ryotwari*, and that successive Governments have persistently done nearly everything in their power to prevent such oppressed ryots improving their position by joining tea estates, on which I maintain, without fear of contradiction, they would, if they were willing, live such a life as I have described in earlier pages. I am going fully into this matter, because I am anxious to show how grievous and criminally unjust Government has been, not merely in negatively refusing to facilitate planters' recruiting operations, but for not systematically organising emigration from the overcrowded districts of Bengal and Southern India, when they knew full well, both that there was a great need of labour in the tea districts, and that there was no room, nor means of sustenance, for a large proportion of the people in locali-

ties from which planters wanted labour. I do not mean
to support my case by any doubtful data, or by state-
ments which—perhaps with some reason—might be
thrown back upon myself, as an incorrect version of
affairs, resulting from a limited knowledge of the subject. When in Assam and Cachar, I frequently inquired
for, and noted, such information as was obtainable from
coolies, regarding the condition of agriculturists in their
respective localities; but I confess that the information
given me was so awful—I can use no other word—that
I thought my informants were treating me to what
Americans call "tall talk and a big thing in yarns," so
accepted what I heard *cum grano salis.* I thought, too,
that possibly my interpretation was excessive, and that
the terms used represented lesser or greater quantities
in the Bengal districts than they did in my own. But
now, sad as is the admission, I find I was insufficiently
informed! Had it been the reverse, in the face of the
more accurate information which I shall give, I should
have abandoned my own notes. The data to which
I allude is obtained principally from the London
Statesman, a journal edited by a good man—sometimes
called in India the "melancholy pessimist"—who, for
a quarter of a century, has been striving to obtain
equitable rule for England's great dependency; and the
article in question—"The Peasantry of India"—is from
the pen of a well-known contributor on Indian matters
to the first London journals, and whose name is a
sufficient guarantee for accuracy. I refer to Colonel
Robert Osborn. I believe I may say, without implying

culpable ignorance, and, I hope, without giving offence (which I should exceedingly regret doing), that from the force of circumstances, and, to a certain extent, the biassed press of India, tea-planters, as a rule, are not in a position to know the terrible phases of life which exist amongst native agriculturists in most parts of India outside the tea districts. I have said that Government has been grievously and criminally unjust in not helping such agriculturists to the tea districts, where there existed a remunerative market for labour. To support this, I cannot avoid giving lengthy extracts from the journal mentioned ; and I believe that in doing so I shall be adding to the knowledge of tea-planters in India and tea proprietors at home, as to the actual condition of the Indian peasant. While I hope to show, before closing this chapter, that the extracts so given bear upon the subject, should any reader consider them excessive, I would ask him to believe that I feel the point at issue to be so important, and know my authority to be so good, that I feared erring on the side of insufficient corroboration to what I have said of the Government action in the labour question.

In England, if a too severe sentence is pronounced by a magistrate on a small boy, there will always be found a Member of Parliament to speak of the matter in the House of Commons, and so bring it to the notice of the Government and the country ; and this representative interest holds good in all matters increasing in importance from the somewhat trivial illustration given. But there is no such thing in India A man with a grievance writes to one of the daily papers, and he can do no more—or, rather, it is wiser of him to do no more, for as a rule he suffers for petitioning the official in whose province the matter in hand really lies. If official notice be taken of the letter in the newspaper, a process of circumlocution ensues, and the Government official nearest to the subject of complaint is called upon for a report. Giving one unfavourable to the Government is playing with edged tools; and the usual result is that the highly-paid officials representing Her Majesty in India, soothe themselves with the belief that they are administering manifold blessings to Indian natives, and that there is nothing wrong. Indeed, I think I might almost with accuracy say that the official mind is such as to consider itself capable of performing absolutely anything, excepting to make a mistake. The London *Statesman* says :—

" A young civilian or a young lieutenant is no sooner landed in the country than he deems himself better fitted to discharge any duties whatsoever than any man of the two hundred millions of human beings who are the natural and rightful owners of the country. Very rarely indeed does this conviction fail him as he rises in the service. In most cases it grows stronger, for as he rises he encounters less and less contradiction. To our countrymen in the East, India is merely the ' milch cow ' whence they are to obtain sustenance sufficient to enable them to return to their native land. The only way to effect this with expedition is to stand well with the powers that be. Clearly, then, the schemes and ideas of these 'powers' are not to be subjected to a rude and unsympathetic criticism by subordinate officials, they must be accepted implicitly, as the revelation of a superior wisdom, in closer neighbourhood to the fountain and source of absolute truth. In this way a strange kind of false conscience is developed in the minds of British bureaucrats in India. It may be designated an 'official conscience,' the primary law of which is not fealty to truth, but what is called 'loyalty to Government.' This 'loyalty to Government' is set forth as having in it something grand and heroic, like the charge of the Six hundred in the Valley of Death,—

> ' Theirs not to reason why,
> Theirs not to make reply,
> Theirs but to do or die,'—

the somewhat important distinction being, unfortunately, ignored, that while the Light Brigade rode into the jaws of death, the devotees of the 'official conscience' are riding only with high emoluments into the enjoyment of large pensions. The 'men of light and leading,' the Lieutenant-Governors, Chief Commissioners, and Members of Council, who distribute honours and emoluments, naturally love to surround themselves with those in whom this 'official conscience' is most highly developed in preference to all others among the sons of men. These are the men who can be trusted to 'carry out orders,' who, as they assure us, 'take an interest in their work,' and who are perpetually burning incense for the delectation of the 'men of light and leading.' As

for those fallen natures who perversely believe, and
insist upon pointing out, that India is not a place
wherein administrative infallibility regulates the destinies
of the best of all possible worlds,—these are consigned
to a doom fit for such dispositions. They are excluded
from the official Paradise, and are sent forth to study
repentance, and develop, if they can, the ' official conscience ' in malarious and remote stations, which have
been known to bring back many an erring and rebellious
spirit to walk in the straight path of ' loyalty to Government.' Surrounded thus by satellites,

> ' For ever singing as they shine,
> The hand that made us is divine,'

a great Indian official regards himself as being in wisdom
superior to Solomon in all his glory. He will undertake
with a light heart the vastest schemes of legislation, the
most sweeping social rovolutions, and record the glorious-
ness of his achievements in his own official reports.
True it is that these achievements, for the most part,
are allowed to bear very little fruit. His successor has
his own crotchets to carry out, his own desire for distinction to be fed ; and amid the hosannas of *his* satellites
' loyal to the Government,' he too frequently begins by
uprooting what his predecessor has planted, and sowing
his own crotchets in their place. But though all things
else change in India, there is one thing that never
changes, and that is the issue of roseate reports setting
forth the achievements of each successive Governor-
General or Lieutenant-Governor, as the case may be.
It is the publication of these reports which has wrought

that deep-seated impression, which must be effaced before any real good can be done, that our administration in India has been a constant passing on from one successful and benevolent achievement to another. A belief more erroneous it would be difficult to discover among the errors and superstitions of humanity.

     *   *   *   *   *

" I cannot, of course, in the space of a brief article, give the record of *all* our failures ; but I choose that particular matter in which we might have achieved our greatest success, had our administration of India been marked by those excellencies which are generally believed to be its leading characteristics. I mean, of course, the condition of the agricultural population. Almost all the wealth that there is in India is obtained from the cultivation of the soil. The bulk of our revenue is derived from the land. It is, therefore, a primary interest, as it is a first duty of such a Government as ours, to have special regard for the prosperity and well-being of the agricultural classes. And in no particular have we been wont to contrast our rule with that of native rule so largely in our own favour, as in our dealings with the land. Our fixed and equitable assessments have, so we have declared, enhanced the value of landed property. Our great public works have enormously increased its productiveness ; and the order we maintain throughout India has given security and peace to the ryot and his family. Under the benign protection of the British Government, they can enjoy the fruits of their toil in unmolested quiet. There is not one of these beliefs which is not delusive. Our dealings with the land have been more completely destructive of all ancient proprietary rights than was the Native rule which preceded our own. Our rigid and revolutionary methods of exacting the land revenue have ground the peasantry down to the lowest extreme of poverty and wretchedness, and the decrees of our law courts have been the means of laying upon them burthens heavier far than any they endured in times earlier than our own.

* * * * *

" Sir Robert Egerton, the Lieutenant-Governor of the Punjab, in the discussion on the Deccan Ryots' Relief Bill, expressed himself as follows (the italics are mine) :—

" ' The circumstances which have led to its being introduced seem to me *to be of such general prevalence throughout India*, that the mode in which they are to be treated in the Deccan may possibly form a precedent in other parts of the country. . . . There are parts of the country in the Punjab, as doubtless there are in every Presidency, where the rainfall is uncertain, and the crops precarious ; yet in all those parts of the country the Government has introduced its revenue system, which obliges the peasant proprietor to make payment of a fixed sum at fixed times, as Government revenue ; and the Government has imposed most stringent conditions in regard to the realisation of this revenue. *It seems to me that but too little stress has been laid on this cause, which must in a great degree contribute to, if not entirely originate, the indebtedness of the Deccan ryots. The ryot who has*

*become indebted to a banker is obliged to pay the Government
demand in cash; to procure that cash he has again to resort
to the money-lender; and as long as the Government demand
regularly comes upon him he is obliged to go again and
again to the money-lender, in order to procure cash to
meet it.'*

" The condition of the Deccan ryots has become so
abnormally miserable, that the cry of their distress has
reached even the careless ears of the British public.
. . . In the foregoing extract from Sir Robert Egerton's
speech, we have the assurance of that experienced officer
that it is the rule throughout India, rather than the
exception.

" Mr. C. Crosthwaite, in describing the revenue
system by which the agriculturist is forced into the
clutches of the money-lender, says :—

" ' Anyone who has gone, about the middle of April,
from Calcutta to Meerut, must have noticed the various
stages of progress of the harvest as he passed upwards.
Below Benares, the fields are all bare and brown. The
corn is in the threshing-floors; most of it is already
trodden out. As the traveller goes northward, more and
more fields of standing wheat and barley meet his eye ;
the stocks of gathered grain become smaller and fewer.
When he reaches Allyghur, it will seem to him that
the sun must have gone back, and the season changed.
The crops that were rich and golden yesterday are
lighter and less ripe to day. Hardly a field is cut. If,
when he reaches Meerut, he leaves the train and passes
into Rohilkund, he will find the wheat still green, and

the harvest-time two or three weeks to come. If the
traveller is a stranger . . . . will he not wonder to
learn that the Government of these countries collects
its rent from one and all at the same time; that the
peasant whose wheat is still standing and green, and the
man whose corn is already trodden out and dressed,
have both to pay their rent on the same day ? . . . Yes,
we think a man would have to search long and far before
he found a more apt illustration of " How not to do it,"
than is to be seen in our system of collecting the land
revenue. If it was our object to make the pressure of
the revenue as severely felt as it could be, how better
could we proceed ? . . . We find that the harvest time
varies from the end of March to the end of April. We
select a day that barely gives time to the peasantry to
reap and sell their crops in the most forward districts,
and make it rent day for all. *Where the harvest is earliest,
we drive the farmers to throw their produce into the market,
and make the fortunes of the dealers; where the harvest is
latest, we forestal it altogether, and compel the peasant to
borrow his rent from the usurer. . . . The result is that the
people are enslaved to the usurer.* And to make the matter
worse, the exorbitant interest which he got when there
were no courts, and when his chance of getting the
principal back was very small, is secured to the money-
lender by all the power of the British Government.'

" It is worth while to follow in some detail the process whereby our agriculturists are enslaved to the
usurer. Under Mr. Crosthwaite's competent guidance,
we can trace it step by step. He takes an ordinary

peasant, and goes through a year with him to see how he gets on :—

" ' It is the beginning of October. He has six acres of land. Three of them are under autumn crops, and three are ploughed and ready for wheat and barley. The next thing is to get the seed. . . . In a big village hard by lives a fat Marwaree, who has the custom of all the country-side. Off to him hies our cultivator, with a dozen others on the same errand. For his three acres he requires, in round numbers, three maunds of seed (a maund is eighty pounds). Wheat is now selling for thirty pounds and barley for forty pounds the rupee. The Marwaree, therefore, books him as follows:—

				R.	a.	p.
Two maunds of wheat	.	.	.	5	5	4
One maund of barley	.	.	.	2	0	0
Total	.	.	.	7	5	4

Our friend then returns home with his three maunds of seed, and his debt of Rs. 7.5.4. He is now busy, sowing his spring crops, and looking after his autumn harvest, none of which is yet ready to gather. October, however, has still a week to run when . . . rent-day has come round. The first instalment is due. The landlord has come for his rents. What is our cultivator to do ? If he cannot pay, the landlord will distrain, and distraint means ruin. . . . The end, then, is that about fifteen days after he borrowed the seed, our friend is on his way again to the Marwaree. This time he wants cash. The whole country-side is then wanting cash ; all at the same time ; all for the same purpose ; all because their crops are not ripe and their rent is due. . . . He lies down that night with a heavy load of debt—Rs. 7.5.4 for seed, and Rs. 8.3.3 for rent. He and his wife talk it over before they go to sleep. Between them they make out that the debt comes to Rs. 15.8.7. But the interest—they cannot count up that. Let us see what it will be. It is universally the custom to recover the advances made in April for seed at the harvest time. The interest charged is at the rate of 50 per cent. per annum. . . . Now, our friend borrowed in October for seed Rs. 7.5.4. Let us see what he will have to pay in April. First, if he pays in money, he will have to return :—

					R.	a.	p.
Principal	.	.	.	.	.	7	5	4
Interest	.	.	.	.	.	1	13	4
	Total	.	.	.		9	2	8

But April is a long way off, and he has no time to think of it. He must, however, repay the money he borrowed for rent, and that soon. Such loans are given for a month only, and interest is charged at the rate of one anna per rupee. . . . So about the 20th of November, the cultivator has to find the sum of Rs. 8.11.6 to repay the loan of Rs. 8.3.3, that he took to pay his rent a month before. In a day or two he has also to pay his second instalment of Rs. 8.3 3 to enable the zemindar to meet the revenue demand of December. But at this time he has not so much difficulty, if the season is good, in finding the money. Well, we need not visit our friend again until his harvest is ripening early in April. . . . Down comes the zemindar again. There is another revenue instalment due on the 15th of May. He must get in his rents a month or a fortnight before. The cultivator has to find Rs. 8.3.3 again. Again he has to go to the Marwaree, and borrow the amount at the same moderate interest of 75 per cent. per annum.'

"In this detailed manner, Mr. Crosthwaite follows one of our Indian cultivators throughout the year, making out that, if all goes well, the man will have about twenty rupees wherewith to support himself and his family for more than six months. And he sums up as follows :—

"'Under the most favourable circumstances, the cultivator must borrow to pay half his rent, and pay interest for one month at the rate of 75 per cent. per annum. Out of every Rs. 100 of rent, Rs. 50 are borrowed, and Rs. 3.4 paid as interest to the money-lender. The revenue of the North-West Provinces is about four million pounds sterling; the rental cannot be less than seven millions. Therefore, in round numbers, about three millions are borrowed every year, and *one hundred thousand pounds paid as interest by the cultivators*. . . . All this burden is simply thrown on the peasantry by the system of taking the rent before the crops are harvested. . . . It appears, then, that by our system of collection, in the most favourable circum-stances, at least one hundred thousand pounds sterling of the produce of the land are made over annually to the money-lenders. *This, however, only represents a portion of the loss actually caused to the peasantry ;* for it is seldom that things go so smoothly as we have supposed them ; and the share of the money-lender in the produce is probably much more than the sum we have named.'

" The reader after perusing the foregoing will not fail to understand how it is that the state of things has been brought about which is described in the following paragraph from a letter of a district officer addressed to the Government of the North-West Provinces, during the terrible famine of 1877–78 :—

" ' In the whole division, the difficulty which presents itself now is this. *The poorer class of cultivators, the ploughmen and labourers, cannot get food except with great difficulty.* The money-lenders close their advances to the cultivators, and the labourers have no work to do. The Banias (*i.e.* money-lenders) are in the habit of feeding the poorer class of cultivators on the strength of, and on the security of, the crops on the ground; whenever there is little or no crop sown, or when the crop sown is endangered by drought, the Banias close their money-bags, and refuse food or its equivalent. *The people are then thrown on their own resources, which are nil.*'

" In other words, the North-West cultivator is the serf of the Bania . . . then perishes in the manner described in the following extract from an official report, dated 1878 :—

" ' Whole families were carried off by one fatal meal. There is a weed called *batua,* which seems to be resorted

13

to a great deal by people in distress, though it is a terribly dangerous food. . . . The general opinion was that so long as a man could get salt to mix with *batua*, and not less than four chitacs (eight ounces) of grain to add to it, a long period could be tided over safely ; but salt was said to be indispensable, and at widely distant points I heard the same expression—" Those who died were those who could not get salt to eat with their *batua*." With or without salt, however, diet of nothing but *batua* for four or five days was, so they said, more than the strongest could stand.'

" But this is the way in which we govern India. So long as the administrative machinery will work at all, our leading officials resolutely shut their eyes and ears to its increasing crankiness, extracting such comfort as they can from the reflection that, in all probability, they will have left the coach before the final and hopeless breakdown. The primary object and desire of ninety-nine out of every hundred Englishmen in the Indian service is to obtain a pension and leave the country. The Indian official is, literally, a hireling who careth not for the sheep whom he is expected to tend. His object is to earn a livelihood, not to redeem a ruined people. His official position, as well as his feelings, are unaffected by either the censure or the approval of those over whom he is set to rule.

*   *   *   *   *

" The land settlement, as it exists to this day in Bengal, Behar, and Orissa, originated, as most people are aware, in a giant act of confiscation. . . . The consequences which ensued constitute, perhaps, the gloomiest episode to be found in the history of British India. Large tracts of land were depopulated, and tenanted only by wild hogs. As late as 1852, the following is a picture drawn of the Bengal ryot by one of his own countrymen :—

" ' In Bengal, the ryot will be found to live all his days on rice, and to go covered with a slight cotton cloth. The demands on him are endless. This prevents the creation of capital, and prolongs the usurious money system. Bengal is noted for the exuberance and fertility of the crops; but the present condition of the ryot is miserable. His monthly expenditure is from one and a half to three rupees, or from three to six shillings ; but there are not five out of every hundred whose annual profits exceed Rs. 100 or £10. . . . He lives generally on coarse rice ; and pulse, vegetables, and fish (a mere drug in Bengal) would be luxuries ; his dress consists of a bit of rag and a slender sheet ; his bed is composed of a coarse mat and a pillow ; his habitation a thatched roof upon supports; . . . he toils from morn till dewy eve ; he is a haggard, poverty-stricken, wretched creature. Even in ordinary seasons, and under ordinary circumstances, the ryots fast for days and nights from literal want of food.'

" This being the testimony of a Native, may be suspected of exaggeration; I add, therefore, the evidence of an indigo-planter, of the same date :—

" ' I question if the ryot is better housed, or better clothed, or better fed, than he was fifty years ago ; he is

13

always in debt, and always in need, and always liable to be oppressed by any man who has power over him. . . . The poorer classes in Tirhoot are even worse off than they are in Bengal. A Bengal ryot has always a tenure of land, which he cultivates at a perpetual rent; but in Tirhoot the ryot has no position; he has not a bit of paper which gives him any right to hold his land longer than the proprietor chooses to allow him. . . . The district of Mymensing, which embraces an extent of land 5,000 miles square, is supposed to contain 800,000 inhabitants. I do not believe there are twenty individuals who possess from £10,000 to £20,000; the greater part of the proprietors are all in debt; the ryots are all in debt; and their debts are generally incurred to exacting bankers. I have known in my experience hundreds of ryots paying 60 per cent.'

" If space allowed, it would be easy to add to these testimonies others of the same kind to almost any extent. But the utter wretchedness of the peasantry in the Lower Provinces is a fact that few will care to dispute.

" The Magistrate of Patna, recently reporting on the condition of the people of Behar, says :—

" ' The expression, " living from hand to mouth," has assumed for me a more definite and tangible, though less satisfactory, meaning than it ever had before. I have been into and over the houses of hundreds of the poorer classes, and have seen how they live and what they eat. *I could not have believed, had I not seen it for myself, how abject is their poverty.* . . . Many of them do not know what it is to have two meals a day; and most of them do not know, when they rise in the morning, whether they will get one full meal or not. *Wages have remained as before, while the prices of all kinds of food have increased.* Over-population seems to be an effectual bar to any further material improvement that might otherwise be brought about by increased means of communication, by education, and other similar means.'

"To this distressing picture we add Mr. O'Donnell's official report on the condition of the people in the district of Sarun:—

" 'It is, however, a fact that the average size of the farms does not exceed five beegahs (a beegah is rather more than an English acre), and that seven persons, according to the census, constitute a household. The average value of the crops produced in one year, taking good land with bad, on a single beegah is Rs. 25, of which Rs. 3 is payable in rent. Therefore, amongst the poorer classes (that is, some 600,000 persons), a family has to subsist on Rs. 102 a year, or only a rupee and four annas each a month—*i.e.* a little more than two shillings a month. Yet even this condition represents a state of things much more favourable than half of the poorer classes, or 300,000 persons, can obtain. Tens of thousands of them have not more than two beegahs of land.

" 'There are, besides, the landless day-labourers, who number from 10 to 15 per cent. of the inhabitants of every village. How they continue to subsist in years of scarcity . . . . is a more difficult question than most people are prepared to answer. The fact is, that the possessors of a larger kind of farms, with areas of from fifteen to thirty beegahs, *know the importance of protecting this class alive, and also of preventing them from emigrating through distress, and give them just enough food to keep body and soul together.'*

" The testimony of Mr. Toynbee and Mr. O'Donnell is abundantly confirmed by Sir Ashley Eden, the present Lieutenant-Governor of Bengal. He writes as follows : —

" 'In the . . . report of the Commissioner of the Bhangulpore division, a lamentable account is given by the sub-divisional officer of the state of things in the Banka sub-division ; two-thirds of which are leased out in farms to non-resident speculators, while, in the remaining one-third, at least half of the landlords also are non-resident. The farms usually run for seven years, and are only renewed on the payment of a heavy and increasing premium, which falls entirely on the ryots. *The tenants are said to have no rights, to be subject to the exaction of forced labour, to illegal distraint, and to numerous illegal cesses*, while the collections are made by an unscrupulous host of up-country (bailiffs). There can be no doubt whatever that the combined influence of zemindars and land speculators *have ground the ryots of Behar down to a state of extreme depression and misery.'*

" Leaving Behar, I will pass on to Orissa. What do we find to be the state of the peasantry here ? I quote the testimony of an experienced Civil officer. He calculates that a ryot in tolerably comfortable circumstances, after the sale of his crops, and the payment of rent, may find himself in possession of Rs. 57, with which to support himself and his family during the year—say ten shillings a month. This is not a large income to subsist upon, but the ryot is very far from retaining the entire amount undiminished. There prevail in Orissa a multitude, which no man can number, of what are called 'illegal cesses,' but which are very regularly levied, none the less, and these are described by our Civil officer as follows :—

" ' The zemindar comes first with his demand for his four annas here, and six there ; so much for a son's marriage, so much more for a daughter. The universal Festival of the Car, in which the unwieldy *ruth* of Juggunath is dragged half a mile along a road, in order that it may be dragged back again the week after, is made the occasion of a levy of one rupee a head from all the peasantry of a populous estate. This levy will produce five thousand rupees, of which barely five hundred will be spent on the purpose for which it was ostensibly raised. Then the zemindar has had to pay seventy rupees income tax, and forthwith *tikkhus* is collected at two annas in the rupee from every cultivator. Or the magistrate has made a Ferry-fund road through the estate, and though the zemindar has received ten times the value of the land in compensation, yet he finds it necessary to recoup his imaginary losses by taking one anna in the rupee from all his tenants. But beside these general and financial measures there are also special and personal inflictions. A neighbour's cattle may have eaten half a field of paddy, and the ryot carries off the offending cattle to the pound, whence they are only released on payment of four annas a head. Off goes the owner of the cattle to the zemindar to complain, and by dint of a judicious present secures his interference. The ryot who so rashly impounded his neighbour's cattle is seized, brought up, and made to pay double the Government fine. . . . By these means, supplemented by the zealous action of a horde of naibs, gomashtas, peons, and dalals (*i.e.* servants of the zemindar engaged in rent-collecting), and completed by the Brahmins, whose dole and presents must on no account be left unpaid, our typical ryot will be lucky if he save in the course of the year twenty rupees out of his fifty-seven. . . . Such is the picture of a man removed above the lowest grade of poverty. But this lowest grade, what of it ? What of the man who tills with borrowed bullocks his little patch of one or two acres, whose wife, clad in one filthy rag, scarcely sufficient for decency, labours at unwomanly tasks during the long day to add a few farthings to the scanty store, and who, beat with fatigue, and prematurely old from want and exposure, may be seen at nightfall picking the tasteless leaves of wild spinach from the margin of the fetid tank to eke out the unwholesome meal of coarse rice, which must suffice her and her starving family ? Not even their squalid hut, with its forlorn inhabitants, escapes the lynx-eye of the *piyada* (zemindar's cess-collector). They must pay their quota to swell the flowing stream of extortion ; there is the lean cow, sell that and pay ; there is one brass drinking-vessel, he will take that in lieu of the demand.'

" This terrible picture of the life of an Orissa peasant appeared some years ago in one of the Calcutta journals, and it had the effect of inducing the Bengal Government to institute an official inquiry into the levy of ' illegal cesses.'   It was discovered that the zemindars in the district of Balasore were accustomed to exact from their tenants no less than eleven ' illegal cesses,' levied at fixed periods, and seventeen ' casual exactions on special occasions.'   The collector at Balasore described the process as follows :—

" ' Some zemindars take even more than these ; but the above, though not exhausting the list, are the principal.   They are not all taken in all estates, but many of them are universal.   In addition to this, several zemindars are in the habit of making their ryots supply them with cloth and other articles at rates far below the market price.   *Khilwan Sing, who is by far the worst of all, lends his ryots one rupee's worth of rice, at a time when prices are high, say eight seers for one rupee, and at a time when prices are low, after harvest, he takes one rupee's worth of rice, say sixty-four seers, from them, thus getting sixty-four seers for eight lent, or eight times the original quantity.   This he defends as quite fair.* . . . It appeared to me that all these zemindars were lamentably and surprisingly ignorant of the state of affairs existing in their estates.   Most of them leave the management of details to their subordinates or agents, a class whose rapacity is notorious in all parts of India where they exist.   The zemindar only knows that when he wants money he tells his agents to raise it from the ryots under some pretext or other, and raised it is accordingly. . . . I may also add that the condition of the ryots . . . is miserable in the extreme. Their houses have not been repaired for three years; they have barely enough cattle to plough with; they are scantily clothed and insufficiently fed, and from sheer want many of them are now working as coolies on canals, though they have enough land to support them, if they were only allowed to enjoy the fruits thereof.'

" Let us now turn from Orissa to Bengal proper . . . thus described by a Bengal Civilian :—

" ' The zemindar and ryot are as king and people; they are as monarch and subject. What the zemindar asks, the ryot will give ; what the zemindar orders, the ryot will obey. The landlord will tax his tenant for every extravagance that avarice, ambition, pride, vanity, or other intemperance may suggest. He will tax him for the *kheeraki* of his naib, for the salary of his ameen, for the payment of his income-tax, for the purchase of an elephant for his own use, for the cost of the stationery of his estabhshment, for the cost of printing the forms of his rent-receipts, for the payment of his expenses to fight the neighbouring indigo-planter, for the payment of his fine when he has been convicted of an offence by the magistrate. The milkman gives his milk, the oil-man his oil, the weaver his cloths, the confectioner his sweetmeats, the fisherman his fish. The zemindar fines his ryots for a festival, for a birth, for a funeral, for a marriage; he levies black mail on them when an affray is committed, when one man lives clandestinely with his neighbour's wife, when an abortion is procured. He establishes his private pound, and realises five annas for every head of cattle that is caught trespassing on the ryot's crops. . . . The cesses pervade the whole zemindari system. In every zemindari there is a naib (deputy), under the naib there are gomashtas (agents), under the gomashta there are piyadas (bailiffs). The naib exacts a perquisite for adjusting accounts annually, at two pice, or sometimes one anna, for every rupee he may collect. The naib and the gomashtas take their share in the regular cesses; they have other cesses of their own. The piyadas, when they are sent to summon defaulting ryots, exact from them four or five annas a day. It is in evidence before the Indigo Commission, that in one year a zemindari naib, in the district of Nuddea, extorted ten thousand rupees from his master's ryots. It is within our own knowledge that, quite lately, a zemindari naib received a *salaami* (*i.e.* congratulatory present) of one thousand rupees. . . . This system of cesses has eaten, like an incurable disease, into the social organisation of the country. An energetic Government might have grappled with the question, and succeeded in abolishing a system which, though forbidden by law, yet flourishes in undisturbed luxuriance; yet no one raises a hand on behalf of the ryots; no one speaks a word in their interest. . . . It seems almost as though they were doomed never to be emancipated from their present degrading life.' "

Such is the testimony to the condition of the Indian ryot. I would ask the reader to remember that (as

Colonel Osborn says in closing his article) these particulars are not those of the belief or experiences of the *Statesman* staff, but extracts from the reports of Government officers, who, by reason of the high positions they occupied, in thus showing-up the misery of the Indian peasantry, had no need to fear retribution for telling the unpleasant truth. It may happen that this book will be seen by civilians who believe only in the unalloyed happiness and prosperity of Her Majesty's subjects in India. Let me impress upon any of these, that the representations here made are those of their own faction—the Lieutenant-Governor of Bengal, the Lieutenant-Governor of the Punjab, and other high officials; and I think I may reasonably add, that it will be useless to say that the facts given are inaccurate. Had they been brought to public notice only as the evidences of the *Statesman* writers, they would have been scouted in most official circles in India; but, as it is, it seems to me that they must be accepted—or else the high officials mentioned be charged with misrepresentation, and the Government service admitted, by members of it, to be liable to gross inaccuracies—an admission which, I imagine, but few civilians would care to make. It will, therefore, be quite useless to ignore these official testimonies, notwithstanding their exceeding unpalatableness.

Now, I believe I may say that the state of things here shown up will very greatly surprise the tea-planting community. The majority of the planters at the present moment are men who have gone from England to join tea properties, and their Indian experience has been exclusively a tea experience. In this way, their knowledge of the condition of Indian natives has necessarily been formed only by the condition of the tea estate cooly, and they would have been able only to believe that, considering his habits and needs, this individual was exceedingly well off, and it is a cause for no surprise whatever that such a belief should be held. I think I may say that, because of this, tea-planters, as a body, have been very warm supporters of the (I hope now partly exploded) theory of the comparatively blissful existence of the peoples of India, as subjects of the Queen-Empress. In so far as experiences in the tea districts go, the British rule in India is decidedly very beneficial for the natives; but after the reports I have quoted, I need hardly say that this does not apply very much farther afield.

Given, then, that the official reports are accurate. I have not confined the selection to reference to Bengal, from which place planters mostly look for labour, and which, also, seems to be in a worse condition as regards the position of the ryot to the zemindar than most of the other places mentioned. But I have purposely given reference to other parts of India—Oude, Behar, Orissa—to show, in thus reviewing several reports, that Sir Robert Egerton was perfectly correct when remarking in his own, that "the circumstances which led to its (the Deccan Ryots Relief Bill) being introduced, seemed to be of such general prevalence throughout India."

Tea-planters have been considered brutal, and unfit to be trusted with labour, unless under periodical Govern-

mental supervision ; they have been opposed by successive Governments, and compelled to spend hundreds of
rupees for labour when tens should have sufficed ; they
have been harassed on every side, and negatively considered conscienceless in their treatment of coolies ; and
now here, under the direct auspices of the Government
that has hindered them, there is revealed, by the
reports of the officials of that very Government, a state
of things far worse than that which obtains in Ireland at
the present moment, and a condition of virtual bondage
of the ryot in relation to his zemindar, which is un-
equalled by the servility of the Turkish peasantry under
the corrupt yoke of the Ottoman Empire. Where
Government has been making it annually more costly
for tea-planters to obtain labour, where stringent, and
even more stringent regulations have been passed,
building up still greater difficulties around the labour
supply, there has existed for the ryot—the man the
planter wanted—a life of chronic starvation, of misery
and wretchedness awful to think upon, a style of clothing well nigh too scanty for decency, and abominably
foul, a mental and physical bondage to the zemindar
and Marwaree, who were countenanced by Government
in foreclosing on mortgages effected at 50 and 75 per
cent. per annum interest—countenanced by the Government which compelled the wretched ryot so to mortgage
his holding, through not waiting the maturity of his
crops for the payment of his rent—and which, on the
testimony of its own officials, has been making the life
of the ryot, even in non-famine times, a misery and a

curse to himself, and certainly to the Government which ruled him, which withheld consideration for his position, and sanctioned the then unavoidable bondage to the usurious Marwaree, a blot, a disgrace, and a crime. And this has been the average life of the ryot in times when his harvests have been favourable. His condition during a famine visitation has been short and simple—death. Such have been—such alas! are—the results of the actions of an enlightened Government, which was most particular in legislating for coolies when they were leaving the inferno of their own homes—like which, because of the starvation-bondage to the Marwaree or zemindar, there was no other place—the Government which neglected the people when they were near at hand and in their native places, neglected them even until, as famine reports show, they died by millions, without a hand being put out early enough to help the weaker of them. And now that they are wanted by men who will readily do everything for them, the enlightened Government, proving the old truth that absence makes the heart grow, oh! so very much fonder, rushes into legislation, becomes suddenly aware that when in the service of responsible agents coolies really must be looked after, and lays down rules as to dress and sanitation *en route*; and as the poor wretches have been starved thus far in their existence (*vide* reports quoted) when under Governmental supervision and paying rent to the Government, in a truly Pecksniffian spirit the same Government now says, "Feed my sheep," draws up a dietary scale for feeding coolies on the steamers, which causes them to die by hundreds every year, because the food is too rich for their debilitated stomachs (such is the medical testimony), which debility has come about when the people were being rack-rented by an enlightened Government, or made over to the tender mercies of the Mawaree or the zemindar. Such is the Government that has opposed the planter and well-nigh baffled him at every struggle for labour, and that has feared he might not treat the people fairly. Such has been the whited sepulchre of a bureaucratic Government, which, being outside seemingly fair and pure, was inside —in its own work—full of corruption and all abominations.

I turn now from noticing these Government reports, to the summary of Parliamentary business as reported in the London daily papers on August 19th, 1881.

"The Marquis of Hartington, in reply to Mr. O'Donnell, said that it was the case that, according to the report for 1879 on coolie emigration in Assam, the mortality rate amongst indentured coolies in two districts exceeded 8 per cent., and 9 per cent. in another. Indeed, in two gardens, it was considerably higher during the second half of the same year. The average death-rate of the district was 5·68 per cent., which, although a considerable improvement over several other years, was still a high rate. It had been pointed out by the Secretary of State to the Government of India that, with a view of lessening the evil, *efforts should be made with a view of improving the condition of the coolies.*" (The italics are mine.)

It would seem from this that tea-planters are beset by the authorities both in England and India. " Efforts be made with a view of improving the condition of the coolies." May not tea-planters (in all meekness, as becomes them), suggest to the authorities—wherever they may be—that a little consideration, and a few efforts to improve the condition of the ryot in almost every part of India, would be to more purpose than legislating for people who are infinitely better off than when in their own country, and who have all things they could reasonably desire ? " There are none so blind as those who will not see " ; and here is the enlightened Government rushing into laws for people who are now well looked after, and living in actual comfort and prosperity, but who were grossly neglected and overlooked in their own country, and overwhelmed in the misery and wretchedness sanctioned by Government, when they were in their own homes. How beneficial might be the result, if Government would cease squinting at the imaginary mote in the tea-planter's eye, and study the beam in its own. " Improving the condition of the coolies "! Would that it were possible to get some disinterested person to report on the respective conditions of ryots paying rent to Government, and coolies working for tea-planters, as a basis for ascertaining *where* existed the need of " improving the condition of the coolies." I write thus, because there is absolutely no parallel in the tea districts to that which is officially reported to be the state of affairs in many parts of India. Where, as has been shown, ryots rise in the morning in

14

all uncertainty as to whether they will have one full meal
during the day or not, where they make up the existence
allowance of food with wild spinach, or are thrown back
upon deadly *batua*, in the tea districts they have rice
provided at a given rate, under compulsion from the
Government, and if the bazaar rate is less than that
stipulated in the agreement, they get their grain from
the bazaar.   Thus, Rs. 3 per maund being the agreement price for rice, when it costs more outside, coolies
look to the factory, and when less, go to the bazaar or
villages. There is no difficulty for them as regards food ;
and fish and vegetables are plentiful.   If they are sick
and quite unable to work, the factory feeds them.   As
regards clothing, remembering that Bengalis patronise a
scanty garb, the tea districts certainly do not show
(amongst imported coolies) the clothing represented by
" a rag too scanty for decency." Certainly cleanliness is
often wanting where clothing is ample ; but against the
people who wear the *minimum* amount of clothing, many
may be found who dress well.   At the times of various
festivals, coolies come out in most elaborate costumes,
and with umbrella, turban, and shoes complete ; their
children often are decked with silver ornaments, and their
women nicely clad.   These are tea-estate *coolies* ; people
who in their own country had not a soul to call their
own.   As regards houses, the average Bengali is easily
pleased.   In the reports mentioned, his home has been
described as " a shelter upon supports " ; in the tea
districts it is a healthy, rain-proof house, built on high,
well-drained land, and repaired when needing attention.

And then pay-day—the day that to the Indian ryot means anxiety and heart-sinking and a visit to the dread Marwaree ? In the tea districts it is all the other way. The coolie, having done his work, goes to his Sahib and draws his pay ; pay-day to the coolie being one of receipt and not of disbursement. I have seen new coolies who were of the labouring, and not of the cultivating, class in Bengal, on receiving their first month's pay, look at it in a way so vague as to indicate a want of comprehension. Likely enough they have never before had so much money at once to call their own; they have earned it, only they have never received it. Many other points show up in the cooly's favour. There are no famine times in tea. The cooly has only to do his work to receive his pay, grow fat, and save money. Drought, zemindari taxation, Marwari usury, dying cattle, gomashtas, piyadas, Juggernath cess, rent-day, seed-time, and harvest— all these things that mean, at the very least, anxiety to the general Indian ryot, do not enter at all into the life of the tea-estate cooly. He has no rent to pay ; and if his house need repair, there is no occasion for him to trouble himself about it—it will be done for him. When he is sick, the doctor attends him ; and even should he die, there will be no expense to his relatives for his burial. How much of this can be said for ryots paying rent to their zemindar or to the Government ? How much representation is required to show that coolies are infinitely better off in the tea districts than in their own homes, and that *planters' employés do not need legislation, as do the people who pay Government rent* ?

14 *

Now as to the death-rate. This is one of the corner-stones of Governmental interference in the planter's labour question. The Marquis of Hartington says that the annual rate of mortality in Assam is 5·68 per cent., or, say, 51 per thousand. I cannot at the moment place my hand upon a newspaper cutting I somewhere have filed ; but I know that in the north of England, or in Scotland, the death-rate varies from 27 to 31 per thousand. I firmly believe in the sacredness of life, and that the existence of each living soul--unless man pervert his life—is essential and dear to its fellows, equally among all nations.* Consequently I take it that coolies on tea estates have something more to live for than merely the convenience of their employers, and that, for either reason, their life is valuable, and should be protected. The Assam mortality rate proves an equivalent of five deaths to three in some parts of the United Kingdom. Taking into consideration the fact that one place possesses (or ought to) all the advantages of sanitation and a healthy climate, it seems to me that there is reason for very general satisfaction in knowing that deaths in Assam are not far more numerous. When it is remembered that all persons in India— no matter of what colour—are liable to sickness more

---

* Perhaps I had better explain this. I say " essential and dear *to its fellows*." I do not mean that the lives of, say, the Assam tea-planters are essential to Nagas ; but that (say) a Naga father is as essential to his Naga children, as the tea-planter, as a son, is to his father's happiness. This is the essentiality of kindred.

frequently, and with less hope of recovery, than in England, surely the proportion of five to three is by no means excessive, and it ought not to form any barrier or obstacle to planters' labour operations. When in Assam I frequently tried to find out, but without success, whether any return was ever made of the mortality in villages, or amongst Europeans. All that I was able to ascertain was that there was no such return. Now, if 9 per cent. of death-rate (which I think is the garden closing percentage), result in a factory being abandoned and much money and labour lost, why should not village mortality returns be called for, and the places shut to settlers in a like event? As far as my own inquiries went, village death-rates seemed considerably in excess of those of tea-factories; but, strange to say, Government does not step in and turn the villagers out. It seems a paradox—but when natives live in swampy places and have no medical attendance they are allowed to do as they please without any inquiries being made as to their well-being or otherwise; but when tea-planters do their utmost to make coolies' habitations healthy, engage doctors and spare no cost in medicines, then Government steps in, calls for returns, and says that unless the death-rate is kept within a certain percentage, the factory will be closed. Yet all the while, often enough, on the boundary of tea gardens, where the high land ceases, villagers live and endure all the ills that flesh is heir to, and die off like Norfolk Howards under somebody's powder. Or if several European managers die at a factory, or one leaves after another through the unhealthiness of the place, Government does not hear of it, or hearing, takes no notice. The first operations of tea estates must necessarily be unhealthy for all concerned; but an increasing industry ought not to be checked because of the first inconveniences. The European risks his life for his salary; it is surely no greater hardship for the cooly to work on the same terms. It would be as well, perhaps, if Government would remember Indian wars in thus obstructing planters' progress. People have cried out a great deal about the expenditure of money in the late Afghan war, but not many of them have cried out in like manner about the awful waste of human life; and the few who did so cry out did not cause the war to be stopped. War, and its inevitable mortality, is legitimate when under the direction of a Government—mortality amongst coolies, obtained at considerable cost, and working indirectly in the interests of commercial peace and prosperity, calls forth the interference of the Government, which may shut up a garden. The legitimacy of war is a wide problem, and hardly bears on the labour question; so I will say nothing more of it, excepting that if Indian wars have been considered justifiable with the results obtained, occasional heavy death-rates in the tea districts ought not to be detrimental to the planters' interests, because the work which, perhaps, results in the death of several coolies, is virtually benefiting those who remain. Every acre of land cleared and planted with tea in India helps to reduce the natural unhealthiness of the climate; and where gardens are opened in particularly unhealthy districts, it would really be wiser to encourage their rapid extension, and so materially lessen the unhealthiness, than to shut them up and retain them as dens of malaria, to vitiate the atmosphere all around them.

In the Parliamentary Report I have elsewhere quoted (August 19th, 1881), the Marquis of Hartington said: "It was proposed, amongst other things, by a Bill before the Bengal Council, to extend the maximum service of coolies to five years, and this was one of the recommendations made by a Commission which had recently reported on the Bengal Emigration Act." This is certainly a step in the right direction. I believe I shall be correct in saying that West Indian planters have for a long time received East Indian (Bengal and Tamil) coolies on five-year agreements; and it seems strange that tea-planters should have been restricted to a three-years' contract, when the coolies were so much nearer their homes. Five-year agreements ought to act satisfactorily for all concerned.

The present conditions of obtaining coolies, and the red-tapeism connected with their journey to tea localities, is extremely far-fetched, and is almost devoid of any real good. Anxious as planters always are to do their utmost for labourers, it would be strange if they did not feel that as the cherished *protéges* of Government, a great deal of unnecessary fuss is made with coolies, especially in the districts where they are recruited. I would here notice the vast difference existing between the Government stipulations regarding Indian coolies moving from one part of their own country to another, and the requirements for emigrants leaving England. As a rule, wherever there is a good field open for emigrants, the home Government gives all the aid in its power to persons thinking of going to it. Agents are appointed to represent the place, advertisements are inserted in the papers, and in most parts of the kingdom the post-offices exhibit notices regarding it. If a man be anxious to settle, he can do so with the greatest ease as regards official supervision; indeed, the action of the Government is merely to see (through its agent) that the man is a fit one to go abroad, and forthwith a passage is given him at a reduced rate. He has not to go before a magistrate to be questioned, and frightened, and registered, and vaccinated and passed on to another official, &c. &c. A code of laws has been passed for the conduct of affairs on emigrant vessels, reports have to be furnished, and an inspection made at the port of destination; but all men and women are perfectly free to go whithersoever they will. If Government consider such regulations as now exist sufficient for emigrants going, say, thousands of miles from home, surely the same might suffice for Indian coolies going only a few hundreds, and not out of India! While I do not think slightingly of cooly life, I must say that it is a far easier thing for a cooly to set up advantageously as a "stranger in a strange land" in the tea districts, than for an European to do so in the Colonies. The Indian Government has a food scale for exporters of coolies to keep to, and calls for reports from medical officers in charge of labour batches, as is the case in English emigrant ships; but the local nonsense of registration is confined to India, and used with people who are only going to another district of their own country. I have several times endeavoured to ascertain as to what practical good this district registration and signing and countersigning of recruiters' licenses was. It avails the planter nothing when seeking to recover absconding coolies. The countersigning magistrates, too, are sometimes very arbitrary. Cases are on record of recruiters' agreements being cancelled on the ground that they entered into them to work on the factory named, and not to travel about looking for labourers. Is not this metaphorically straining at gnats ? Using a recruiter at all represents double expenditure ; for his labour is lost to the garden, and his travelling expenses incurred.

There is good reason for planters looking to the Government of India for help in the industry in which they are engaged, for in addition to individual and personal interests, they are doing good work for the country, in developing its resources at the peril of their health. It should be remembered, also, that as a rule the position of the planter is a singularly unprotected one. He lives away in the jungle, with very little save the fact of being an European to protect him, and year after year he thus lives a life of risk and danger. An illustration of the manner in which he can be attacked—annihilated, I was nearly saying—was recently given in the horrible murder of Mr. Peter Blyth in Cachar. The Nagas simply walked into the factory at night, killed the manager and eleven coolies, and went away. The majority of tea estates might be assailed as easily; and tea-planters virtually form a frontier guard for the people in the plains, and are thereby assisting in maintaining peace in their respective districts.

In previous pages I have dwelt at some length on the dreadful condition of the ryot in various parts of India. I have also tried to show the injustice of the Government in taking the view they do take of the tea industry. In Chapter VIII. I have said that it was not logical to condemn anything as bad without showing the substitute. I therefore wish to show that the Government has it in its power to help the ryots who are suffering in their respective districts, and to help tea-planters at the same time. The condition of the ryot is bad enough to call for more extensive legislation than my knowledge of India is adequate even to suggest; but it seems to me that in the tea districts there is open a field for labour from which much relief might be obtained. I do not recommend the ryots flocking indiscriminately to the tea districts; for emigration in such a form would be unwise. I do not even recommend tea estates as an *alternative* labour-field for unsuccessful ryots, because their number is greater than could possibly be maintained in the tea localities; but I certainly do mention tea districts as *palliative* fields, in which a great demand for labour exists. Now, I think the *general* character of the official testimony will have shown in how many places there has existed labour which was both surplus and unprovided for. But even more than what may be almost called the chronic distress, do the famines of past years show

what fields have been open for obtaining labour for the
tea districts, had the Government been active in putting
into force one of the first axioms of political economy—
to save life.   These famines have been—in the North-
West Provinces in 1860 ; in Orissa in 1866, when the
awful scarcity first aroused the attention of the British
nation to these terrible visitations ; in 1868 upwards
of a million human beings perished of hunger in Raj-
pootana ; in 1870 there was scarcity, verging upon
famine, throughout the North-west ; in 1873 occurred
the well-known famine in Behar ; in 1877 famine carried
off a third of the population of Madras and Mysore, and
extended to a portion of the provinces under the Bombay
Government ; in 1877-78 the *Khureef* harvest failed
throughout the North-west, and upwards of a million
men and women perished during the winter months of
cold, disease, and hunger.

In the palliative degree to which I have referred, I
think some thousands of people who have died in the
course of these dreadful calamities might have been
saved, and stlll alive, had Government been vigorous in
taking them out of the afflicted districts, instead of keeping them there on an existence allowance.   Although so
doing would possibly have increased the death-rate of
tea estates, many lives would have been saved at all
events, and the famine devastations curtailed.   In addition to lives thus saved, money would also have been
saved to the State, in a twofold measure.   Relief during
the famine would not have been necessary ; and the Bills
which are constantly passing through the Council for

distressed ryots and others would not have applied to
those who had left for the tea districts.   Such relief
Bills are constantly being introduced—the Deccan Ryots'
Relief Bill, Jhansi Zemindars' Relief Bill, Oude Talook-
dars' Relief Bill, &c.

In the agricultural districts it is customary for people
who are not of the actual labouring class, to cultivate
land, not as a speculation, but for the maintenance of
themselves and families; and such people, as a rule,
work only for themselves.   Their love for ancestral
holdings is very great; and it generally seems that they
would prefer starving on, to listening to the tea-estate
recruiter's roseate version of how things are in the " *chá
muluk.*"   But, year by year, from the want of scientific
cultivation and the inability of the ryot to manure his
holding, land in many districts is becoming poorer and
poorer, and the condition of the tillers of the soil worse
and worse.   Now, in such circumstances, Government
certainly might use its influence to represent to the ryots
and labouring classes in agricultural districts, that ample
food, good pay, and a total absence of Marwarees and
Zemindars, were obtainable in the tea districts; and
Government might organise emigration for the planter's
benefit.   Central depôts could be established in Calcutta,
and garden agents be allowed to select their men (as is
now the custom with cooly contractors), paying Government the cost of conveyance from the respective districts,
together with that of depôt feeding.   The result of this
would be, that where at the present time families are
huddled together in numbers which their small patches of

land cannot possibly properly support, with some of the people removed, those remaining would have a better chance of a more cheerful existence, as regarded a sufficiency of food. Also, as famines, unfortunately, seem to be becoming somewhat regular in their courses, nearly each year bringing one of some extent or other in one part of India—with the population thus thinned by Government emigration, the distress in the different districts would not be so great, as the available food would be divided between less people, and where Government aid was given, its recipients would be fewer. At the present time the usual practice during famines is to establish Government relief depôts, and to put the people on to making roads. Now it stands to reason, that if natives know they have only to get badly enough off through famine for Government to step in and feed them, they will sit down with exemplary patience—the joint outcome of debility, laziness, and *kismet*—and wait the advent of Government representatives; and all efforts to persuade people at such a time to leave for the tea districts would be futile. He would be a rare and a very queer Hindoo, who would go from his home to work in a distant locality, when he knew that Government would feed him in his own place if he could manage to keep life together long enough. Then as to roads. Roads are not undivided blessings in agricultural districts; they certainly let the grain carts in when there is a scarcity, but they lead to a market when the famine is over, and the Marwaree has grabbed the ryot's first crop. Where a good road does not exist, there is not much inducement to take grain; but with a good one, crops are easily realised upon.

During the Southern Indian famine, tea-planters made offers to the Government, through the Indian press, to engage coolies who might be landed in Calcutta; but hardly any notice was taken of the matter. People might have been conveyed from Madras to Calcutta by contract for, at most, Rs. 5 per head, and put in good hands, by which their future would have caused no concern; as it was, they were allowed to remain in their homes, and were fed by the Government; and those who live until another famine will have a pretty good notion as to what Government will do for them, if they manage to hold on long enough. I would here just say that I consider it to be the clear duty of the State to provide for people who are starving; but I also believe permanent prevention in emigration to be better than temporary cure by relief bills. In the different famines I have mentioned, Government might have drafted natives from the oppressed districts to Calcutta, for tea-planters' use: they would have been gladly taken. Some of the Madrassi coolies are not particularly well-suited for Bengal tea factories; but I have known them to be gradually built up into useful men. North-west Provinces people, too, are still less so; but it would surely be no worse to make them over to tea-planters on the chance of their living, by having every attention paid them, than to let them remain in their own districts on a much greater chance of dying! Particularly would planters have been glad had labour been thus supplied during the earlier stages of the Behar famine. Of course, in cases of famine coolies being sent to tea estates, a margin would have to be allowed in the death-rate. A short food-allowance often sows the seed of death in a cooly that all after-care and good feeding cannot eradicate.

In all the *thannahs* of districts which are likely to be afflicted by drought, Government might easily order to be put up notices giving particulars of work and pay on tea estates, explaining the Governmental control of the movement, advocating the people's acceptance of the chance, and follow this up by establishing local depôts for collecting the people previous to transference to Calcutta. A few thousands going thus to help tea-planters, even if complete holdings were abandoned, would be as nothing to the revenues of the agricultural districts where millions remained to pay rent ; and where members of families emigrated, they would be well looked after, and in their going be benefiting those who remained; as the land left to their kinsfolk would have fewer people to support.

There is also another way in which Government might help themselves, and planters too. The frequent lay of land in the tea districts—at all events in Assam, Cachar, and Sylhet—is alternate stretches of low land suitable for rice, and high land fitted for tea. (The miasma from the former rises to the latter, and brings out leaf-flushes in the garden, and fever ones in the bungalow.) In many cases, particularly in Assam, there are *enormous* stretches of land well suited for rice, which may almost be said never to have been inhabited. Invariably Assam planters have to obtain rice from Bengal, although on the borders of their grants they have land which, if cultivated, could supply a large part of India with rice. The Assamese have, if any, very little market for grain, excepting that made by tea-estate coolies, and beyond these sales they only cultivate for their own requirements. By working for a few months in the twelve, they get sufficient grain to keep them during the year—a rather different picture from the official reports previously quoted. It would be an easy matter for the Chief Commissioner of Assam to call on each Assistant or Deputy Commissioner in Assam, Cachar, and Sylhet, to obtain from each *Mouzadar* in his district particulars of vacant rice-lands, waste or abandoned. Into these, Government might bring ryots from different parts of India, where people are too thick or the land too poor, and if not disposed to do this for nothing—that is to say, at the expense of the State— the cost of conveyance might be recovered in an assessment per acre (or *poorah*), distributed over three or four years. Assam land is particularly fertile; and under Government auspices, struggling ryots might soon experience as much benefit from emigration as English farmers do in going to New Zealand, Australia, or America. People so brought up would only need to work on their crops for a few months annually; in the other time they would be able to give their services to tea-planters (as Bengali villagers in Cachar do at the present time, on a small scale), and who would be but too glad of their help.

Of course, it will surprise no one when I say that these propositions seem perfectly feasible to myself. If Government would do away with the troublesome routine which at present obtains in the labour districts, and would encourage emigration by organising it, either directly to the planter through Calcutta depôts, or to the vacant rice lands in the tea districts, the loss of rent in one place would be made up by its payment in another, poor land in overcrowded districts would have a chance of improvement, families on it—being smaller—would be better fed, waste lands would be opened out—at all times a desirable event—and tea-planters would be helped. Or looking at the matter exclusively from a planter's point of view, advancement in the tea industry would be materially assisted, by drafting off from oppressed districts a few thousands of folk who now live by starving.

There is now the last point to be noticed in connexion with this question. Coolies arriving on tea estates generally seem very stupid at first. This is not to be wondered at considering the state of bondage in which they have lived. Old coolies on tea estates are sensible, rational men. I never yet knew a cooly who had saved money to be in other respects a fool. Life on tea-factories—the regular food, good pay, and comfortable housing—unquestionably tell most beneficially on the mental construction of coolies. We know the old adage, that a certain class of folk and their money are soon parted. Tea-factory experience shows that matters work conversely, too, and in a marked manner; for a man

15

who certainly seemed nearly allied to a fool on arrival
at a factory, always develops into a sensible fellow by the
time he has a little money to call his own. This result
is surely a good one, and most beneficial, especially
when compared with the servility that often comes of
zemindari labour. The result is open to easy proof; and
it forms, I consider, another link in the chain of good
reason which exists for Governmental countenance to
tea-planters' labour needs.

The Government seems all along to have regarded the
tea industry in a biassed light. It is easy to imagine to
what extent tea-growing might have advanced had there
been fewer difficulties in the way of obtaining labourers.
There is money enough available to extend the industry to far greater lengths, when the labour embargo
is removed; and the increased industry means grist to
the State revenues, which will be in no way inconve-
nienced by financial help. Many people believe that
tea-planting even now is only in its infancy. Let the
Government remove the mill-stone of labour difficulties,
and we shall soon see the infant rapidly advancing into
youth and vigorous manhood, with no uncertain progress.
Prohibitive interference in respect to labour retards the
planter, and withholds available help to Indian finance.
I have endeavoured to show the evil of this, its injustice to all concerned, and a way out of the difficulty
which seems to me to be a very easy one. Knowing
that the subject of this chapter is to the planter more
important than any other, I have not hesitated to express
my opinion to the best of my ability, in plain words,

where occasion seemed to require them. While not wishing to rush into heroics, or to constitute myself the press champion of the votaries of an industry which is old enough to be, if not my father, certainly my very elder brother, I hope I may say that I have endeavoured in the interests of the industry to which I shall shortly return, to show, as it seemed to me, the actual complaint and the possible cure of this important question ; and I trust my diagnosis will prove to be correct, and the treatment recommended be successful.

15 *

CHAPTER VIII.

THE SOCIAL PHASE OF TEA-DRINKING.

" Now stir the fire, and close the shutters fast ;
   Let fall the curtain, wheel the sofa round ;
   And while the bubbling and loud hissing urn
   Throws up a steaming column, and the cups
   That cheer, but not inebriate, wait on each,
   So let us welcome peaceful evening in."

                                    COWPER.

PHILANTHROPISTS of the present day are constantly
seeking to do good by a wholesale condemnation of
alcoholic drinks. It is not unlikely that their case
would be strengthened, and more good done, if they
were to show up the advantages of the various beneficial
drinks of nations. Without questioning the many evils
of intemperance, it must be confessed that platform
oratory on the subject has become almost hackneyed.
Beside which, it is hardly logical, in endeavouring to
benefit people, to give but one side—the evil—of the
drink question, without recommending substitutes and
being equally emphatic upon their merits—seeing that

people must have something to drink. If temperance advocates were to print and circulate as freely as they do pamphlets denouncing strong drink, others based on the same conclusive lines, showing the chemical construction of natural beverages and the advantages of their use, they would aid their cause, and enable people to nourish their bodies partly on scientific principles. Knowledge is the surest preventive against animal indulgences. Interesting pamphlets on the nature and use of tea, placed side by side with the injurious effects of alcohol, would undoubtedly advance the use of the former.

During the last three centuries tea may be said to have been first the representative, and now the national drink of English people at home and abroad. Numerous and wholesome as are many other social and non-alcoholic beverages, tea is the most used, and—from an all-round point of view—the most beneficial. It is a powerful agent in the domestic economy of England, and enters largely into many of the public phases of society. Ministers accept and resign charge of congregations at gatherings of tea-drinkers ; foundation-stones are laid, and theological anniversaries held, in the tea-pot. Philanthropically-inclined people frequently have the germ of their benevolence hatched at a tea-meeting, and little nether vestments and moral pocket-handkerchiefs result from the ascending aromatic incense, and the descending comforting decoction. "Love's young dream " often wakens to its dual fantasy as the drinker's eyes wander over the side of the tea-cup to the bright ones of somebody's sister near at hand. And at that season of the year when nature, in England, has retired within herself, and no longer gives forth her fruits, the many Ladies Bountiful in towns and in villages sally forth with comfort for the needy masses, and distribute little parcels of tea and sugar.

Tea is used as a very general beverage, and is equally a favourite one. Unlike many of the constituents of our dietary system, it holds rank both in the homes of the affluent and the indigent.

"That all classes of the community in this country have derived much benefit from the persistent use of tea, is placed beyond dispute. It has proved, and still proves, a highly-prized boon to millions. The artist at his easel, the author at his desk, the statesman fresh from an exhaustive oration, the actor from the stage after fulfilling an arduous *rôle*, the orator from the platform, the preacher from the pulpit, the toiling mechanic, the wearied labourer, the poor governess, the tired laundress, the humble cottage housewife, the votary of pleasure, even, on escaping from the scene of revelry, nay, the Queen on her throne, have, one and all, to acknowledge and express gratitude for the grateful and invigorating infusion." *

The *Edinburgh Review*, in noticing *The Chemistry of Common Life*, by Dr. Johnston, says :—

"By her fireside, in her humble cottage, the lonely widow sits : the kettle simmers over the ruddy embers, and the blackened tea-pot on the hot bricks prepares her

* *Food Papers.*

evening drink.   Her crust of bread is scanty, yet as she
sips her warm beverage genial thoughts awaken in her
mind ; her cottage grows less dark and lonely, and
comfort seems to enliven the ill-furnished cabin.   When
our suffering and wounded soldiers were brought down
frozen and bleeding from the trenches before Sebasto-
pol to the port of Balaklava, the most welcome relief
to their sufferings was a pint of hot tea, which was
happily provided for them.   Whence this great solace
to the weary and worn ?   Why out of scanty earnings
does the ill-fed and lone one cheerfully pay for the
seemingly unnourishing weekly allowance of tea ?   From
whatever open fountain does the daily comfort flow,
which the tea-cup gently brings to the careworn and the
weak ? ''

In sickness, frequently when an invalid can *fancy*
nothing else, he can *relish* tea : in health, he likes it for
its own merits, and the social happiness surrounding it.
Indian planters will be able to speak of the place tea
holds, when thinking of the fever and ague the most of
them will have passed through.   In our morning meal
it enlivens and starts us fairly for the day: we are
grateful for it on reaching home, tired and exhausted, in
the evening.   In summer we appreciate it as we take it
on our lawns ; in winter, when Nature's face is white
with snow, it is especially welcome by our own fireside.
In palaces and in camps, on land and sea, whether we
are exhilarated with pleasure or saddened with trouble,
tea is the beverage we take to gladly—and beneficially.
We sometimes meet singular people, who dislike fish, or

vegetables, or sugar, or milk, but it is a rare thing
indeed to find anyone disliking tea.   Out of England,
too, the fragrant beverage is a great institution.   The
stockman on Australian sheep-runs lives upon tea,
corned beef, and damper ; and it has been given me as
a fact, by one of the fraternity, that frequently the last
two would scarcely be eaten without the former.   Dismal
and lonely is the stockman's life, and devoid of mental
comforts ; and tea ranks highest in his small list of
creature ones.   In wealthy Russian circles, from early
morning until late at night the brass " Sámává " steams
with the fragrant odour of " Ochai."   The Parisians have
fairly inaugurated the English custom of five o'clock tea.
Social gatherings among our own middle classes, and in
Nonconformist circles, would seem to be greatly wanting
in something were tea absent, even though every other
similar beverage were provided.

The various uses to which tea is put would pronounce
it to be a good-nature drink.   People quarrel over wines
and spirits, but very seldom over tea.   In small family
gatherings the social ice is quite thawed by the time tea
is over, and people are on good terms with themselves.
It is a pity that some of the suburban vestrymen near
London do not begin their meetings with a tea-drinking;
for then, perhaps, some of the ridiculous proceedings
that are recorded would not occur.   People do not bet,
nor challenge each other, when drinking tea, nor even
indulge in strong language *pour passer le temps.*

> " When in discourse of Nature's mystic powers
>   And noblest themes we pass the well-spent hours,

Whilst all around the Virtues—sacred band—
And listening Graces, pleased attendants stand.
Thus our tea conversations we employ,
Where with delight, instruction we enjoy,
Quaffing without the waste of time or wealth,
The sovereign drink of pleasure and of health."

BRADY.

"Tea is no vulgar conjurer, whose aim is to make people stare. It insinuates itself into the mind, stimulates the imagination, disarms the thoughts of their coarseness, and brings up dancing to the surface a thousand beautiful and enlivening ideas. It is a bond of family love; it is the ally of woman in the work of refinement; it throws down the conventional barrier between the two sexes, turning the rude strength of the one, and ennobling the graceful weakness of the other. At the dinner-table there is something almost repulsive in the idea that we are met for the purpose of satisfying the animal necessities of our nature; and our attempts to gild over this weakness by a gorgeous display of plate, crystal, and porcelain, only serves to superinduce an air of stiffness and formality. At the tea-table, on the other hand, although one may likewise eat, he does so without the gross sensation of hunger, while he who has no appetite at all, is spared the smell of smoking viands. In drinking, his excitement is seen, not in the flushed face, extravagant laugh, and confused ratiocination, but in an unconscious buoyancy of spirits, a rapid but clear flow of ideas, and a kindliness, amounting to a warmth of regard, for all around him."

In some Eastern countries tea-drinking is the opening

ceremony of hospitality, and the traveller may feel safe for the time and fairly hopeful for his mission, when he sits on his host's carpet, drinking tea.

According to the testimony of many travellers, it would seem that the bulk of mankind require something in the way of a stimulant. Wherever this is tea, civilisation is in full progress; for tea seems to lead to refinement. Just as we almost naturally look for elegancies at the tea-table, so we may, on a broader ground, look for pleasant social courtesy, and refinement of surroundings, among tea-drinking peoples. Particularly would this seem to be borne out by the Japanese. The poorest lads are educated, and the girls are instructed in embroidery as well as in scholastic branches. If we look at tea-drinking communities, we shall find, almost without exception, that this rule of refinement holds good. It is believed by the Chinese that they were led to commence and perfect their beautiful manufactures in drinking-vessels as necessary adjuncts to the beverage they delighted in. Savage nations, and non-tea-drinkers, are contented with horns, leaves, calabashes, and rude metal vessels from which to drink.* In the history of various national tumults, we find no mention of the use of tea at the time being, but we do find frequent record of the unbridled use of alcoholic drinks. Tea-drinking seems quite inconsistent with any disorder or coarseness. The studious, romantic, and orderly nature of the Chinese has been accounted

* *Chambers' Journal.*

for by themselves to their extensive use of tea; and
where we read of mutinies and rebellions among that
great people, we find that they have invariably originated amongst the poorest or wildest of them—people
who, cheap as tea is, were unable to purchase it, and
for their drink had to be contented with decoctions of
leaves other than those of the tea-plant, the use of
which was quite devoid of any beneficial result.   In thus
writing, I remember a verbal picture drawn some time
since by a good, public man, of the difference in the homes
of thousands of London artizans on Saturday night when
beer was drunk (and the men, too), and the Sunday
afternoon, when tea was used.   The incident now occurs
to me for the first time, and confirms my belief of the
beneficial effects of tea.   It may be asked " How is it
that in England, being a tea-drinking country, so much
crime, depravity, and brutality still exist ? "   It is
seldom, indeed, that these are found anywhere save in
cases of the excessive use of intoxicants ; or, if not so,
where a parallel exists with the Chinese circumstances
before mentioned, that the people get imitation tea,
which does them harm rather than good.

Tea takes its place in domestic economy as a great mental stimulant, and as an adversary to alcohol.   Dr. Lewis
says that in moderation it strengthens the stomach, is
good against indigestion, nausea, and diarrhœa, refreshes
the spirits in heaviness and sleeplessness, and counter-
acts the operation of inebriating liquors.   That tea is
actively regarded as a rival of alcohol, in gratifying the
taste without injuring the health or maddening the brain,

is proved by the establishment of "Coffee Public-houses," where tea is the principal liquor sold, and which houses are unquestionably doing great good in poor districts of London and its suburbs. Diverse as are the opinions of medical men as to the merits of tea, it is impossible not to believe that, where excess is not indulged in, much benefit is obtainable from an infusion of wholesome leaf. This belief was supported by the *Edinburgh Review* many years ago :—

"Most people are now aware that the chief necessity for food arises from the gradual and constant wearing away of the tissues and solid parts of the body. To repair and restore the worn and wasted parts, food must be constantly eaten and digested. And the faster the waste, the larger the quantity of food which must daily be consumed to make up for the loss which this waste occasions. Now, the introduction of a certain quantity of theine into the stomach lessens the amount of waste which in similar circumstances would otherwise take place. It makes the ordinary food consumed along with it go farther, therefore, or more correctly, lessens the quantity of food necessary to be eaten in a given time. A similar effect, in a somewhat less degree, is produced by the volatile oil ; and, therefore, the infusion of tea, in which both these ingredients of the leaf are contained, affects the rapidity of the natural waste in the tea-drinker in a very marked manner. As age creeps on, the powers of digestion diminish with the failing of the general vigour, till the stomach is no longer able to digest and appropriate new food as fast as the body wears away.   When such is the case, to lessen the waste is to aid the digestive powers in maintaining the strength and bulk of the weakening frame. It is no longer wonderful, therefore, that tea should be the favourite, on the one hand, with the poor whose supplies of substantial food are scanty ; and, on the other, with the aged and infirm, especially of the feebler sex, whose powers of digestion, and whose bodily substance have together begun to fail."

We are able, therefore, to reasonably desire that the use of tea may extend ; and that India, being foremost in the production of pure leaf, may receive such public support as will make the future of the industry very bright and prosperous.

APPENDIX.

ORIGINAL HOME OF THE TEA-PLANT.

At a recent meeting of the Royal Botanic Society, a quantity of tea-seed of three special varieties having been received direct from China, and an interesting collection of growing plants of several varieties of both Indian and Chinese teas from the Society's greenhouses being on the table, Professor Bentley took occasion to say that although tea had been cultivated in China for perhaps thousands of years, it is probable that in early times the plant was introduced into China from India, *it being really a native of Upper Assam.* All botanists now agree that many varieties of the tea-plant are derived by long culture from one common origin; and not only so, but the endless varieties of teas known to commerce depend more on the age of the leaf and mode of manipulation for their individual properties, than to the variety of plant from which they are gathered. The Secretary said that although the tea-plant had been so long under cultivation in China, it had comparatively only recently been introduced to England. It was of easy culture, and being a true Camellia, the treatment under which the *Camellia Japonica* was now so generally grown would suit it, and probably, with a little attention from our leading horticulturists, as interesting varieties in the flower might be obtained as is now seen in the leaves of the tea, or in the flowers of the Camellia.—*Home and Colonial Mail*, February 18, 1881.

The foregoing was forwarded to the author by the kindness of the Editor of the *Home and Colonial Mail*, when the Appendix proof-sheets had been returned to the printer. This Botanical *testimony* singularly bears out the author's *theory* as to the home of the tea-plant.

LAND RULES OF THIRTY YEARS' LEASE.

1 to 2 years	. . .	No rent.
3 to 6 ,,	. . .	3 annas per acre.
7 to 10 ,,	. . .	6 ,, ,,
11 to 20 ,,	. . .	8 ,, ,,
21 to 30 ,,	. . .	1 rupee ,,

CALCUTTA AGENTS OF TEA CONCERNS.

Agra Bank.
Andrew, Hoyes & Co.
Ashburner & Co.
Balmer, Lawrie & Co.
Barry & Co.
Begg, Dunlop & Co.
Bennertz & Co.
Blechynden, R.
Carritt & Co.
Colvin, Cowie & Co.
Cresswell & Co.
Derrick, —, Esq.
Dollet & Co.
Doyle & Co.
Duncan Brothers & Co.
Elliot & Co.
Fergusson & Co.
Finlay, Muir & Co.
Gillanders, Arbuthnot & Co.
Gisborne & Co.
Gladstone, Wyllie & Co.
Grindlay & Co.
Henderson & Co.
Hoare, Miller & Co.
Jardine, Skinner & Co.
Kernot, Dr. C. N.
Kerr, Tarruck & Co.
King, Hamilton & Co.
Land Mortgage Bank of India.

Lloyd & Co.
Mackinnon, Mackenzie & Co.
McIntosh & Co.
McKillican & Co.
McKnight, Anderson & Co.
McNeill & Co.
Moran & Co.
McTavish & Co.
Owen, T.
Reid, R. J.
Robert & Charriol.
Robinson, G. H.
Schoene, Kilburn & Co.
Sen & Co.
Shaw, Finlayson & Co.
Simpson & Co.
Smyth & Co.
Staunton & Co.
Steel & Co.
Struthers & Co.
Sykes & Co.
Teil & Co.
Thacker, Spink & Co.
Thomas & Co.
Watson & Co.
Whitney Brothers & Co.
Williamson, Magor & Co.
Young & Co.
Yule, G.

THE districts in which tea is grown in India at the present time are :—Assam, Cachar, Sylhet, Darjeeling, Chittagong, Neilgherry hills, Chota Nagpore, Kangra, Kumaon, Sikkhim, Nepaul, Dehra.

I take these two lists from the Map and Index recently compiled in India by Mr. F. Linde, whose large experience, extending over many years, is a guarantee for the greatest accuracy obtainable. Areas are increasing almost daily, and agencies changing frequently. With this allowance, at all events for the purposes mentioned in this book, the work may be taken as thoroughly authentic. It is procurable in London from Messrs. D. J. Keymer and Co., 1, Whitefriars Street, Fleet Street, at the following rates :—

	£	s.	d.
Unmounted in sheets	2	2	0
Mounted on linen in book-form . . .	2	12	6
,, ,, and rollers . . .	2	12	6
Index containing district areas, names, marks, agents, managers, and assistants of estates in the different districts, alphabetically arranged, and with an interesting Essay on Tea in India, 52 pages .	0	10	6

MAP OF INDIA.

Stanford's portable Map of India, 86 miles to inch, 29 inches by 33 inches, mounted on linen, coloured politically, showing rails, canals, mountains, &c., in case. 8s. Stanford and Sons, 55, Charing Cross, S.W.

300-ACRE GARDEN.

Operations begin by say	Land planted.	Growth of Garden.		Bearing area.	Remarks.
	acres	acres		acres	Two-thirds of garden will be planted when first return is gathered.
April 1st, 1881	50		April 1st, 1881		
,, 1882	50	100	,, 1882		Half the area will be yielding when planting is finished.
,, 1883	50	150	,, 1883		Between the last planting and full bearing, three years would elapse, in which all factory improvements might be completed—felling timber, making roads, erecting houses, &c.
,, 1884	50	200	,, 1884	50	
,, 1885	50	250	,, 1885	100	
,, 1886	50	300	,, 1886	150	
			,, 1887	200	With a sufficient labour-staff in sixth year, and machinery obtained for manufacture, no expenses would need to be afterward incurred for labour.
			,, 1888	250	
			,, 1889	300	

At a rough estimate, this garden, if of good *ját* plant, might be valued at two-and-a-half lakhs of Rupees.

16

OUTFIT.

It will seem somewhat strange, I doubt not, to begin this head with " Teeth." Persons with questionably sound teeth should have them examined before leaving England for the tea districts. It is a rare thing to find Dentists in the tea localities, and the general—poultry and rice—diet is particularly troublesome for unsound teeth. Chills or feverish symptoms generally affect broken or decayed teeth, and, as a rule, a man has to be his own dentist, or suffer inconvenience until he reaches Calcutta.

Arrangements should be made, before leaving home, for the regular despatch of a good weekly newspaper—one containing plenty of English news rather than a journal of politics, as Parliamentary information is always provided by the Indian press. Monthly magazines or class journals which have been regularly read at home, will be found doubly interesting in India, where literature is somewhat scarce.

Any business of this kind, engaging passages, forwarding goods, receiving packages from India for delivery to friends at home, or any kind of agency business, can be arranged for with Messrs. D. J. Keymer & Co., 1, Whitefriars Street, Fleet Street, London.

A good lamp is a *sine quâ non* to comfort in the tea districts. Hinck's Duplex is largely used in India, and Messrs. Osler & Co. manufacture a very good reading-lamp. The former, or one similar, is better for general purposes ; and a small bed-room lamp will prove useful. All, however, must be specially made for India, in being *punkah-proof*, else they will prove almost useless. London prices for lamps are lower than Indian ones. A large supply of wicks, several spare chimnies, and one or two globes, should be also taken, as breakages are certain sometimes to occur, when, unless there are reserve articles, considerable inconvenience is likely to be caused in obtaining substitutes from Calcutta.

Kerosine oil is procurable in Calcutta in half-maund (41 lbs.) tins, in wooden cases ready for shipment.

White clothes and mosquito-curtains are cheaper, as a rule, in India than in London. With a pattern provided, native tailors will make a good number of jackets and trowsers in a few days.

Night-gowns are substituted in India by sleeping-suits—loose drawers and a jacket. Indian outfitters in London understand this item.

A breech-loading smooth-bore is the most useful all-round fire-arm for the tea districts, although rifles are occasionally handy.

Revolvers are very little used, as planters do not go about their work armed with shooting-irons, and coolies are not partial to being shot. If revolvers are wanted at all, it is in the Texas fashion—real bad ; and if one is not to hand, it is never wanted afterwards. It is awkward to get ammunition into India, and should be sent only through a shipping agent who understands the routine. All requisites for sport are obtainable in Calcutta. Advice, being very cheap, leads me to caution the uninitiated against trifling with fire-arms. It is a very inconvenient thing to shoot a native by accident, and pardonable only by its sequel, to shoot oneself. I unfortunately know of both these cases happening, and another of one planter mortally wounding another. This is not sport.

All mediums of occupying leisure profitably should be taken out. Amateurs in photography will find their knowledge greatly in demand. No valuable or prized books should be reserved for use on the voyage. Shipboard literature is generally "*pro bono publico*," and afterwards for the stewards. The climate of the tea districts plays sad havoc with books. A good way to take them out and keep them in India, is to have a tin-lined case fitted with shelves and folding-doors, like a book-case, tin-lined, and fastened with a good lock. The case should be bound with hoop iron, and covered with sewn canvas.

Photographs suffer much in India. Albums may be well protected in flannel bags, which can be tastefully made of scarlet flannel edged with blue silk. Or if my taste is too quiet, try yellow flannel edged with green baize.

It is a great mistake to discard old cloth clothes before going to India. They are very useful in the cold weather, on wet days, and during fever bouts. Jackets are more useful in jungle-life than coats.

The more flannel is worn, in shirts, trousers, jackets, and sleeping-suits, the better. Silk and wool is also a very comfortable material to wear. "Oxford" shirts (generally called Jute in

India) are much worn in the tea districts, but nothing can equal flannel. All shirts should be made with turn-down collars attached, of a size larger than those worn at home, and a breast pocket or pockets (outside).

Pipes are articles of general use amongst tea-planters; and as the climate (or some other cause) conduces to their speedy decay, spare ones should be taken.

I would recommend that all necessary articles be taken from London, as the cost is less than in India. A dinner and breakfast service for six or nine, ironmongery (enamelled), plated ware, and cutlery of medium quality only (as natives believe in sand for cleaning), glassware, filter, &c. &c.

Boots require to be mentioned particularly. They never wear out in India, but break out, the work giving way through damp and rain, and, consequently, are rendered useless. Good, strong, nailed shooting-boots, with fixed tongues, and of the stoutest make procurable, should be taken, and several pairs of them; and a large supply of laces, and Dubbin (or any similar good preparation) will be of great service. A pair of light riding-boots should also be included in the outfit, together with a pair of stout leggings, fastening without springs.

Umbrellas are used for sun and rain. Silk ones are of no particular glory in the jungles; strong alpaca or zanella answers all purposes. London outfitters have very useful umbrellas for the sun—white cloth lined with green, and a light cane handle —which I would recommend.

A mattrass of some kind will be wanted. Coir ones are procurable in Calcutta bazaars at a very low rate; but cork ones are far more serviceable, comfortable, and convenient in travelling. A waterproof sheet to cover same will sometimes be invaluable.

The following are all more or less requisite or useful for the voyage or in India, but cannot be noticed in detail :—

Blankets.	Soiled linen bag.	Shoe-horn.
Sheets.	Scotch cap.	Boot-brushes.
Pillow-cases.	Courier bag.	Despatch-box.
Towels.	Corkscrew.	Stationery.
Table-cloths and napkins.	Flask.	Compass.
	Canvas shoes.	Lantern.

Dusters.	Overcoat.	Clock.
Rug and strap.	Riding-breeches.	Saddle, cloth, and
Easy chair.	Dress suit.	bridle.
Binoculars.	Needles, threads,	Clipping machine.
	and buttons.	

It is unnecessary to enumerate the articles ordinarily contained in a dressing-case, or those in daily wear. A top-hat will not be admired in the tea districts.

All tailors' and hosiers' measurements should be left at home, so that after-supplies of clothing can be obtained.

HEALTH.

Under this head I have very little to say, being quite sure that as many relatives and friends as can possibly squeeze in a word on the subject will do so. All I need say is that excessive eating or drinking in any country is bad, but particularly so in a hot one—therefore avoid excesses. Never bathe shortly after a meal; take as little medicine as possible, and that only when it is needed. Allow Nature to manage itself as long as it can. No one with the least tendency to Rheumatism ought to go to the tea-districts. Avoid the general failing of new assistants of taking to drink—not from the bottle, but from the tea-pot. Could Dickens have seen how young planters generally absorb tea, it is possible that Sam Weller's " mother-in-law," or the young person who drank nine breakfast-cups of the beverage at one sitting, would never have come into notice. Excessive tea-drinking is very injurious. For complete guidance to health, I strongly recommend every assistant to obtain Surgeon-Major Moore's Indian domestic medicine book, published under Government auspices, and obtainable from Messrs. Thacker, Spink & Co., of Calcutta, at (I believe) Rs. 7. 8a. The new assistant will act wisely in learning, as soon as possible, the nature and treatment of cooly complaints.

It is useless to worry oneself about health. Where a decision has been made to go to India, a negative acceptance has been given to whatever health may follow; so the wisest thing to do is to be careful of oneself, and wait until sickness arrives, instead of rushing out to meet it.

WEATHER.

The London *Evening News* of November 7th, 1881, said :—
" The Indian Tea supply is likely to be unusually short this
year, owing to the cold weather in Bengal and Assam. Not more
than 48,000,000 lbs. will be available for export." The weather
is a very important agent in the production of tea, although it
can hardly be said to be of primary importance in all respects.
Good weather and poor soil will not result in good tea—although,
for that matter, neither will good soil and bad weather. Old
gardens are very largely dependent upon climatic conditions for
their returns. Wonderful bursts of vigour are sometimes seen in
old bushes during good growing weather, and estimates are
exceeded under such happy conditions. But one thing is certain—
that with the weather unfavourable, quantity and quality of out-
turn are alike affected. When, to some extent, quantity is
absolutely dependent upon the weather, the practice of estimating
for out-turn at the beginning of a season seems quite valueless.

DEATH-RATE.

When noticing the death-rate in Chapter VII., I said that in a
newspaper-cutting I somewhere had filed, the mortality in the
north of England, or in Scotland, was shown to be 30 per 1,000.
Against this, the tea-districts' death-rate of 50 per 1,000 did not
seem excessive. In the *Echo* of 20th January 1882, a letter from
Dr. Allinson says :—" Dr. S. Gibbons reports that High Street,
Whitechapel, is inhabited on the north by the Jews, and on the
south side by Irish and English. The death-rate among the Jews
was 20 per 1,000, amongst the Irish and English 43 per 1,000."
What can now be said of the Indian death-rate of 5 per cent., when
the mortality percentage in the very heart of the metropolis of the
world is shown to be $4\frac{1}{3}$ per cent. ?

GLOSSARY.

Ap hum ko aisa dik det'ta roj bá roj.	You give worry to me like this day by day.
Ap ka gholám	Your slave.
Bádját syces	Fractious or troublesome grooms.
Bágichá	Garden.
Bátua	A weed.
Bhai	Brother (or acquaintance).
Bháng	Indian Hemp.
Burra khannahs	Big dinners (dinner parties).
Burra Sahib	Big Sahib (or the superior).
Chá ka Durpán náták	Historical Mirror of Tea-planting.
Chá muluk	Tea country.
Cutcha	Flimsy—of reed and plaster.
Dák bungalow	Rest-house for travellers.
Dák gharry	Post or travelling carriage.
Darogah	Superintendent.
Dástoor	Custom.
Dik	Worry.
Durwán	Door-keeper.
Gharry	Conveyance.
Ghát	Landing-place.
Gunjá	An opiate.
Gupping	Gossiping.
Hai	Yes (literally, Is).
Hál	Cachar land measurement, about five acres.
Háwá khan'na ko	To eat air.
Hikmát	Dexterity.
Hookum	Command: order.

Hubble-bubble . . .	Hookah.
Jungly-wallah . . .	Jungle resident (literally, individual).
Kamjarï	Routine of work.
Khábar	News.
Kheeraki	Maintenance.
Kismet	Destiny.
Mátwallah . . .	Intoxicated person.
Mem-sahib áp ko salaam det'ta.	The lady gives her salute (compliments) to you.
Mem-sahib hai ? . .	Is the lady (mistress) in ?
Mem-sahib nahin hai, likhin Missee-bábá-logue hai.	Mistress is not in, but the young ladies are.
Mofussil	The wilds.
Mouzadar. . . .	Government rent collector (Assam).
Piyadar	Cess Collector.
Poorah	Land measurement (Assam); about an acre and a third.
Ryotwari	Agricultural community.
Salaami	A present.
Táláp	Salary.
Thánnah	Police station.
Tikkhus	Cess.
Tom-tom	Native drum.
Topee	Hat.

London: Printed by W. H. Allen & Co., 13 Waterloo Place, S.W.

For EU product safety concerns, contact us at Calle de José Abascal, 56–1°, 28003 Madrid, Spain or eugpsr@cambridge.org.

www.ingramcontent.com/pod-product-compliance
Ingram Content Group UK Ltd.
Pitfield, Milton Keynes, MK11 3LW, UK
UKHW042209180425
457623UK00011B/119